The Basics of Cloud Computing

Understanding the Fundamentals of Cloud Computing in Theory and Practice

Derrick Rountree

Ileana Castrillo

Hai Jiang, Technical Editor

AMSTERDAM • BOSTON • HEIDELBERG • LONDON
NEW YORK • OXFORD • PARIS • SAN DIEGO
SAN FRANCISCO • SINGAPORE • SYDNEY • TOKYO

Syngress is an imprint of Elsevier

ELSEVIER

SYNGRESS

Acquiring Editor: *Chris Katsaropoulos*
Editorial Project Manager: *Benjamin Rearick*
Project Manager: *Punithavathy Govindaradjane*
Designer: *Russell Purdy*

Syngress is an imprint of Elsevier
225 Wyman Street, Waltham, MA 02451, USA

Library of Congress Cataloging-in-Publication Data
Rountree, Derrick.
  The basics of cloud computing: understanding the fundamentals of cloud computing in theory and practice /
Derrick Rountree, Ileana Castrillo.
    pages cm
  Includes bibliographical references and index.
  ISBN 978-0-12-405932-0 (paperback: alkaline paper)
  1. Cloud computing. I. Castrillo, Ileana. II. Title.
  QA76.585.R68 2013
  004.67'82–dc23   2013024858

British Library Cataloguing-in-Publication Data
A catalogue record for this book is available from the British Library

ISBN: 978-0-12-405932-0

Printed and bound in the United States of America

14   15   16   17   18   10   9   8   7   6   5   4   3   2   1

Working together
to grow libraries in
developing countries

www.elsevier.com • www.bookaid.org

For information on all Syngress publications, visit our website at *store.elsevier.com/Syngress*

Dedication

"This book is dedicated to my daughter Riley. Every day, you get more and more amazing."

– Derrick Rountree

"To my dear friend Deb. You are my rock."

– Ileana Castrillo

Contents

Contributed Chapters

Chapters 6 and 7, as well as small excerpts from the earlier chapters, were originally published in *Securing the Cloud* by Vic Winkler and *Moving to the Cloud* by Dinkar Sitaram and Geetha Manjunath and are used with permission.

Preface

WHAT TO EXPECT FROM THIS BOOK

Cloud environments are pervasive and can be expected to host at least a portion of every organization's future technology landscape. *The Basics of Cloud Computing* is a guide that will help you navigate the questions that surface when you're considering or embarking on a cloud initiative. The cloud is no longer available only to large companies or those with big budgets; this cost-saving technological alternative is now available to the masses.

At some point, every organization will have to make a decision as to whether they want to take advantage of the cloud. Regular consumers are having to make decisions about whether to store their pictures, music, and data files on their local system or use some cloud provider. So what do you choose? The answer isn't so simple. It all depends on your specific needs and resources available to you. The purpose of this book is to help you make the most informed decision possible in a limited amount of time. We want to equip you with the knowledge you need to make the best decision for your personal circumstances, whether you're an enterprise administrator or a home user.

INTENDED AUDIENCE

This guide is for people looking to familiarize themselves with cloud computing technology. Whether you're simply looking to gain general knowledge or you need to make a decision as to whether to move to a cloud environment, we've got you covered. We'll even help those who have already made the decision to move but need to decide which provider to use.

WHY IS THIS INFORMATION IMPORTANT?

Making a decision to move to a cloud environment should not be taken lightly. For many IT departments and organizations in general, it means a shift in the way they do business. You don't want to take these decisions lightly. It's important that you arm yourself with as much information as you can get before you make your decisions. This book will help you obtain that important information.

STRUCTURE OF THE BOOK

This book is broken into seven chapters. We start with a general introduction to the cloud and the technologies that comprise it. Then we discuss the options that are available when we're looking to implement a cloud environment. Then we guide you through making your decision. After you have made your decision, we cover some of the considerations that must be made in implementing your cloud environment.

Chapter 1 gives you a basic introduction to the cloud and the concepts associated with it. We cover some of the benefits that are driving cloud adoptions. We describe some of the issues and concerns that have some organizations wary of moving to a cloud environment. We also cover how some of these issues and concerns can be alleviated.

In Chapter 2, we review the technologies and concepts that come together to create cloud environments. We cover authentication, general computing concepts, virtualization, and Web development technologies.

Chapter 3 gets into the various cloud deployment models. We cover public, private, community, and hybrid clouds. We look at the benefits and drawbacks of each model. Then we look at the security implications of each model. Finally, we examine what is entailed in maintaining each environment.

The cloud is all about services. Chapter 4 covers the various cloud service models, starting with the three main service models: Software as a Service (SaaS), Platform as a Service (PaaS), and Infrastructure as a Service (IaaS). Then we get into some of the newer service models that have been developed.

In Chapter 5, we talk about making decisions around the cloud. First we describe what you need to consider in your decision whether to move to the cloud. Then we talk about choosing a service model. Your next step is to choose a deployment model. Finally, we go over what to consider when you're choosing a public cloud services provider.

In Chapter 6, we talk more in depth about evaluating cloud security. We look at a framework for doing your evaluation. We cover foundational security, business considerations, and operational security.

Once you have built your cloud environment, you need to run it. In Chapter 7 we cover operating a cloud environment as we describe how to access to the environment, operating procedures, and processes. We also cover efficiency and cost.

We believe the material covered in these chapters will not only solidify your understanding of the cloud, but also help guide you through your cloud implementation. With the cloud, as with most new technologies and concepts, the key to doing it right is to make sure have a good understanding of what you're dealing with. You need this understanding in order to ensure the cloud is right for your organization. Our aim is to make sure you have that understanding.

CHAPTER 1

Introduction to the Cloud

CHAPTER POINTS
- What Is the Cloud?
- Cloud Drivers
- Cloud Adoption Inhibitors: What Is Holding People Back?

INTRODUCTION

The concept of *cloud computing* can be very confusing. In this chapter, we'll start by giving you a general overview of the cloud and the concepts associated with it. Then we will discuss some of the factors that are driving organizations to the cloud. We will close by taking a look at some of the issues that are preventing an even greater shift to the cloud.

WHAT IS THE CLOUD?

There has been a lot of debate about what the cloud is. Many people think of the cloud as a collection of technologies. It's true that there is a set of common technologies that typically make up a cloud environment, but these technologies are not the essence of the cloud. The cloud is actually a service or group of services. This is partially the reason that the cloud has been so hard to define.

Originally, the cloud was thought of as a bunch of combined services, technologies, and activities. What happened inside the cloud was not known to the users of the services. This is partially how the cloud got its name. But that definition has since changed. Providers have realized that although some users won't care about what is going on behind the scenes, many actually do care. This user interest prompted providers to be more forthcoming about what they are doing. In many cases, customers are even allowed to configure their own system monitoring solutions.

1

FIGURE 1.1
The Cloud Conundrum

As with all services, the cloud and the services it offers have changed over time. Most services change very quickly to adapt to customer needs. Think about it: Which services, especially technology-related services, have you used that have not changed over time? Not many, right? If you're a service provider, you have to modify and fine-tune your services in order for them to remain relevant and valuable to your customers. Well, the cloud is no exception. This is where the confusion came in. Each time someone came up with what they thought was a good definition, the services changed. Many thought that once the National Institute of Standards and Technology (NIST) came up with a formal definition for cloud computing, that would be the final word. But, as we've seen, even the NIST has changed its definition over time.

Even with the changes, the NIST definition still remains the standard most people refer to when talking about the cloud. The NIST cloud definition has three main components that we will discuss:

1. Five key cloud characteristics
2. Four cloud deployment models
3. Three cloud service models

Key Cloud Characteristics

A lot of companies and services providers have been trying to cash in on the popularity of the cloud. Many providers claim to offer cloud services, even though they really do not. Just because an application is Web-based does not mean that it is a cloud application. The application and the service around the application must exhibit certain characteristics before they can be considered a true cloud implementation. The NIST definition of cloud computing outlines five key cloud characteristics: on-demand self-service, broad network access, resource pooling, rapid elasticity, and measured service. All five of these characteristics must be present in order for the offering to be considered a true cloud offering.

On-Demand Self-Service

On-demand self-service means that a consumer can request and receive access to a service offering, without an administrator or some sort of support staff having to fulfill the request manually. The request processes and fulfillment processes are all automated. This offers advantages for both the provider and the consumer of the service.

Implementing user self-service allows customers to quickly procure and access the services they want. This is a very attractive feature of the cloud. It makes getting the resources you need very quick and easy. With traditional environments, requests often took days or weeks to be fulfilled, causing delays in projects and initiatives. You don't have to worry about that in cloud environments.

User self-service also reduces the administrative burden on the provider. Administrators are freed from the day-to-day activities around creating users and managing user requests. This allows an organization's IT staff to focus on other, hopefully more strategic, activities.

Self-service implementations can be difficult to build, but for cloud providers they are definitely worth the time and money. User self-service is generally implemented via a user portal. There are several out-of-the-box user portals that can be used to provide the required functionality, but in some instances a custom portal will be needed. On the front end, users will be presented with a template interface that allows them to enter the appropriate information. On the back end, the portal will interface with management application programming interfaces (APIs) published by the applications and services. It can present quite a challenge if the backend systems do not have APIs or other methods that allow for easy automation.

When implementing user self-service, you need to be aware of potential compliance and regulatory issues. Often, compliance programs like Sarbanes-Oxley (SOX) require controls be in place to prevent a single user from being able to use certain services or perform certain actions without approval. As a result, some processes cannot be completely automated. It's important that you understand which process can or cannot be automated in implementing self-service in your environment.

Broad Network Access

Cloud services should be easily accessed. Users should only be required to have a basic network connection to connect to services or applications. In most cases, the connection used will be some type of Internet connection. Although Internet connections are growing in bandwidth, they are still relatively slow compared to local area network (LAN) connections. Therefore, the provider must not require users to have a large amount of bandwidth to use the service.

Limited bandwidth connections lead to the second part of this requirement: Cloud services should require either no client or a lightweight, thin client. First, downloading a fat client can take a very long time, especially on a low-bandwidth connection. Second, if the client application requires a lot of communication between the client system and the services, users may experience issues with latency on low-bandwidth connections.

This brings us to the third part of this requirement: Cloud services should be able to be accessed by a wide variety of client devices. Laptops and desktops aren't the only devices used to connect to networks and the Internet. Users also connect via tablets, smartphones, and a host of other options. Cloud services need to support all of these devices. If the service requires a client application, the provider may have to build platform-specific applications (i.e., Windows, Mac, iOS, and Android). Having to develop and maintain a number of different client applications is costly, so it is extremely advantageous if the solution can be architected in such a way that doesn't require a client at all.

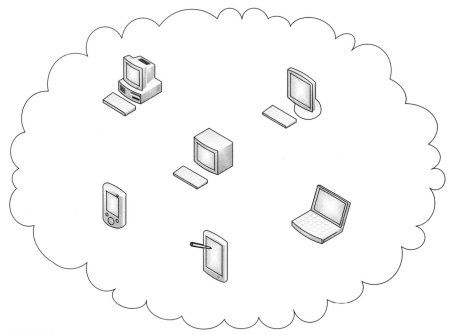

FIGURE 1.2
Broad Network Access

Resource Pooling
Resource pooling helps save costs and allows flexibility on the provider side. Resource pooling is based on the fact that clients will not have a constant need

for all the resources available to them. When resources are not being used by one customer, instead of sitting idle those resources can be used by another customer. This gives providers the ability to service many more customers than they could if each customer required dedicated resources.

Resource pooling is often achieved using *virtualization*. Virtualization allows providers to increase the density of their systems. They can host multiple virtual sessions on a single system. In a virtualized environment, the resources on one physical system are placed into a pool that can be used by multiple virtual systems.

Rapid Elasticity

Rapid elasticity describes the ability of a cloud environment to easily grow to satisfy user demand. Cloud deployments should already have the needed infrastructure in place to expand the service capacity. If the system is designed properly, this might only entail adding more computer resources, hard disks, and the like. They key is that even though the resources are available, they are not used until needed. This allows the provider to save on consumption costs (i.e., power and cooling).

Rapid elasticity is usually accomplished through the use of automation and orchestration. When resource usage hits a certain point, a trigger is set off. This trigger automatically begins the process of capacity expansion. Once the usage has subsided, the capacity shrinks as needed to ensure that resources are not wasted.

The rapid elasticity feature of cloud implementations is what enables them to be able to handle the "burst" capacity needed by many of their users. *Burst capacity* is an increased capacity that is needed for only a short period of time. For example, an organization may need increased order-processing capacity at the end of the fiscal quarter. In a traditional environment, an organization would need to have internal capacity to support this load. Most likely this would mean that there are resources that are always available but are only used a fraction of the time. In a cloud environment, an organization may take advantage of public cloud resources for that short period of time. There is no need to have that capacity always available internally.

Measured Service

Cloud services must have the ability to measure usage. Usage can be quantified using various metrics, such as time used, bandwidth used, and data used. The measured service characteristic is what enables the "pay as you go" feature of cloud computing. Once an appropriate metric has been identified, a rate is determined. This rate is used to determine how much a customer should be charged. This way, the client is billed based on consumption levels. If the service is not used on a particular day, the customer is not charged for that time.

If you are paying for cloud services, you need to make sure you understand exactly which services are being measured and charged for. In a measured service, it's very important that you understand the associated costs. If you don't have a good understanding of the charges, you may be in for an unwelcome surprise.

Cloud Deployment Models

The way the cloud is used varies from organization to organization. Every organization has its own requirements as to what services it wants to access from a cloud and how much control it wants to have over the environment. To accommodate these varying requirements, a cloud environment can be implemented using different service models. Each service model has its own set of requirements and benefits. The NIST definition of cloud computing outlines four different cloud deployment models: public, private, community, and hybrid. We give a brief overview of these here; they are covered more in depth in a later chapter.

Public

When most people think about cloud computing, they are thinking of the public cloud service model. In the public service model, all the systems and resources that provide the service are housed at an external service provider. That service provider is responsible for the management and administration of the systems that are used to provide the service. The client is only responsible for any software or client application that is installed on the end-user system. Connections to public cloud providers are usually made through the Internet.

Private

In a private cloud, the systems and resources that provide the service are located internal to the company or organization that uses them. That organization is responsible for the management and administration of the systems that are used to provide the service. In addition, the organization is also responsible for any software or client application that is installed on the end-user system. Private clouds are usually accessed through the local LAN or wide area network (WAN). In the case of remote users, the access will generally be provided through the Internet or occasionally through the use of a virtual private network (VPN).

Community

Community clouds are semi-public clouds that are shared between members of a select group of organizations. These organizations will generally have a common purpose or mission. The organizations do not want to use a public cloud that is open to everyone. They want more privacy than what a public cloud offers. In addition, each organization doesn't want to be individually responsible for maintaining the cloud; they want to be able to share the responsibilities with others.

Hybrid

A hybrid cloud model is a combination of two or more other cloud models. The clouds themselves are not mixed together; rather, each cloud is separate, and they are all linked together. A hybrid cloud may introduce more complexity to the environment, but it also allows more flexibility in fulfilling an organization's objectives.

Cloud Service Models

When you look deeper into what services can be provided by a cloud implementation, you start talking about cloud service models. The NIST definition of cloud computing outlines three basic service models: Infrastructure as a Service (IaaS), Platform as a Service (PaaS), and Software as a Service (SaaS). We will briefly cover these models here, then cover them more in depth in a later chapter.

Infrastructure as a Service

Infrastructure as a Service, or IaaS, provides basic infrastructure services to customers. These services may include physical machines, virtual machines, networking, storage, or some combination of these. You are then able to build whatever you need on top of the managed infrastructure. IaaS implementations are used to replace internally managed datacenters. They allow organizations more flexibility but at a reduced cost.

Platform as a Service

Platform as a Service, or PaaS, provides an operating system, development platform, and/or a database platform. PaaS implementations allow organizations to develop applications without having to worry about building the infrastructure needed to support the development environment. However, depending on the PaaS implementation you go with, you may be limited in what tools you can use to build your applications.

Software as a Service

Software as a Service, or SaaS, provides application and data services. Applications, data, and all the necessary platforms and infrastructure are provided by the service provider. SaaS is the original cloud service model. It still remains the most popular model, offering by far the largest number of provider options.

CLOUD DRIVERS

The cloud presents people with many new opportunities. Previously, to roll out new applications, you would have to spend a lot of money in upfront costs to get the systems in place and get your staff trained. Now, depending on which provider you choose, those costs can be cut dramatically. The cloud has been a big factor in ushering in this new age of consumerism, or *user-centric IT*. End users don't have to be stuck using applications that they don't like or that don't fit their needs. They can more easily move to a different application that does what they want. It's not seamless, but it's definitely a lot easier than it used to be.

Nowadays, some of the most widely used SaaS applications are customer relationship management (CRM) and enterprise resource planning (ERP) applications. CRM and ERP applications can be very unwieldy and difficult to implement and support. In the past, organizations had no choice but to implement these systems internally. Consequently, they had to deal with all the support and management headaches those systems entailed. Now, with SaaS, many organizations are moving to hosting instances of these applications, saving themselves a lot of time, money, and stress.

System Drivers

There are many system drivers that are steering organizations to the cloud. An organization may want certain system characteristics that they can't provide with their current architecture. Organizations might not have the expertise or funding to achieve certain environment characteristics internally, so they look to a cloud provider to provide them. These characteristics include agility, reliability, scalability, and performance.

Agility

Cloud environments can offer great agility. You can easily reappropriate resources when needed. This allows you to add resources to systems that need them and take them away from systems that don't. You can also easily add systems to expand your capacity.

Internal cloud environments allow you to make better use of your internal infrastructure resources. A cloud infrastructure that uses virtualization can help you increase your density and the percentage of utilization from your infrastructure. As a result, you will be less likely to have systems sitting idle.

Reliability

Building reliability into your environment can be very costly. It usually involves having multiple systems or even multiple datacenter locations. You have to do disaster recovery (DR) and continuity planning and simulations. Many cloud providers already have multiple locations set up, so if you use their services, you can instantly add reliability to your environment. You may have to request to have your service use multiple locations, but at least it's an option.

Scalability and Elasticity

A cloud environment can automatically scale to meet customer needs. New resources can be dynamically added to meet increased usage. This helps in two ways. The increased capacity helps ensure that user needs are met. The fact that resources can be dynamically allocated on demand means that they don't always have to be available, which means you don't need to have systems waiting and sitting idle. These systems still use resources. If you don't need to have the system waiting, you can save on utilization of resources such as power and cooling.

This scalability allows you to better meets your customers' needs. You can quickly add the capacity your customers need for temporary or permanent expansion. You can use an external cloud environment for temporary capacity to provide resources while you expand your permanent capacity.

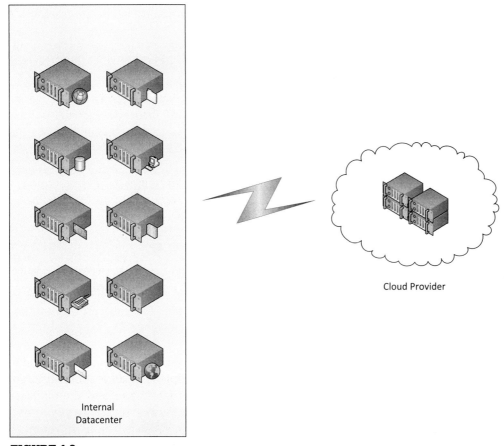

Cloud Provider

Internal
Datacenter

FIGURE 1.3
Burst Capacity

Performance

Performance in cloud systems is constantly being measured and monitored. If performance falls below a certain level, the systems can automatically adjust to provide more capacity, if that is what's needed. The presence of a service-level agreement (SLA) is also a benefit. An SLA guarantees a certain level of performance. If that level is not met, the service provider must generally meet some level of restitution. This restitution is often in the form of a chargeback or a fee reduction. So, although performance itself is not assured, there can be an assurance that the cost of a lack of performance can be mitigated.

Ease of Maintenance

Ease of maintenance can be a very attractive benefit of cloud computing. If someone else is managing the infrastructure and the systems used to provide the service, they will generally be responsible for maintenance. This means several things. You don't have to worry about tracking and staying up to date with the latest hardware and software patches. You don't have to worry about spending time trying to manage multiple servers and multitudes of disparate client systems. You don't have to worry about the downtime caused by maintenance windows. There will be few instances where administrators will have to come into the office after hours to make system changes. Also, having to maintain maintenance and support agreements with multiple vendors can be very costly. In a cloud environment, you only have to maintain an agreement with the service provider.

Security and Compliance

Many experts consider security in a cloud environment to be much tighter than in a traditional environment. The administrators and engineers who run cloud environments don't have to be generalists, as is usually the case in traditional environments. They can focus on securing one type of environment or one type of data. This focus allows the administrators to put more time into coming up with better security measures. In addition, a cloud provider may have more money to devote to solving a particular issue. After all, they will be solving the issue for multiple customers, not just one organization.

Many organizations are looking to the cloud to help ease their compliance burden. Compliance restrictions can put a big strain on your IT environment. They can limit your flexibility and the choices you can make around securing your environment. If you are able to outsource certain functions to an external provider, you may also be able lessen some of the compliance burden of your organization.

Business Drivers

The cloud can help you get applications up and running faster. It also provides improved manageability and less maintenance and enables IT to more rapidly adjust resources to meet fluctuating and unpredictable business demand.

Once you tap into these benefits, you can transform your business into a more streamlined and agile architecture. There are also other key benefits related to cost and consumerism.

Cost

Cloud environments can be a source of reduced cost. One of the biggest cost savings is the transition from capital expense to operational expense. When setting up a traditional environment, the infrastructure and equipment have to be purchased ahead of time. This equipment is usually purchased as part of an organization's capital budget. In a cloud environment, you don't have to worry about purchasing the equipment; you only pay for the service. The cost of the service will usually count against an organization's operational budget. Generally, it's easier to get operational expenses approved than to get capital expenses approved. In addition, traditional cloud environments are built using utility storage and utility computing. These are generally cheaper than more specialized components.

Consumerism

The information technology (IT) landscape is being changed by the notion of consumerism. *Consumerism* is a focus on the needs and wants of the consumer. Consumers aren't bound to a single paradigm; they are free to choose the access methods and applications they want. To meet these consumer needs, IT environments must be flexible. They may need to provide a host of different applications that provide the same function. Having to support this multitude of applications can be very difficult and costly. Using a cloud environment to provide these services can make it a lot easier. Most cloud environments can provide access from different devices such as computers, tablets, and smartphones. They give users the flexibility to access the service any way they want.

Technology is Catching Up

Recent advancements in technology are a big reason the cloud is gaining momentum. In the past, the cloud was seen as a good idea but a pipe dream. The technology wasn't there to make the dream into a reality. The cloud model was lacking key components to make it a viable option. It was expensive to get enough servers to service your customers. After all, you had to have separate servers for each customer. Applications were monolithic and couldn't span locations. Many applications required a larger amount of data to be transferred between the application and the client. The provider would have to do all the servicing. Now technology has been developed that addresses many of these deficiencies.

Virtualization

Virtualization has been a big driver in the movement toward the cloud. In fact, when many people think about the cloud, they think virtualization is a requirement in a cloud environment; but it's not. Virtualization can play an extensive role in a cloud implementation, but it is definitely not required. With virtualization, you are able to host multiple virtual systems on one physical system. This has cut down implementation costs. You don't need to have separate physical systems for each customer. In addition, virtualization allows for resource pooling and increased utilization of a physical system.

Application Architecture

There have also been many changes in the way that applications are architected and designed. Previously, a single application could not service multiple clients. There was no way of preventing one customer from accessing another customer's data or parts of the application. Now multiple customers can access a single instance of an application, but their interactions are segmented.

Applications have also begun implementing service-oriented architectures. SOA allows applications to be broken down into components. These components are accessed individually. SOA allows applications to share components. SOA exposes APIs that can be used by client systems or client-side applications.

Open-source computing allows providers to customize cloud implementation applications such as hypervisors and orchestration technologies to meet their own needs. You start with a base application set, but you can customize the application to fit the needs of your organization.

There has also been increased standardization around Web development. This standardization has led to increase compatibility and interoperability. It has also led to an increase in Web-based development. This means lighter clients.

Bandwidth Increases

Internet access speeds (bandwidth) have increased dramatically. This has increased the overall speed of application access. In many cases, Internet-based access can be comparable to local LAN-based access. Increased bandwidth can mean better response times. This has helped drive an improvement in the usability of Web-based applications.

Driver for Cloud Providers

Over the past few years, the number of cloud services and cloud providers has steadily increased. Not only are there cloud drivers for consumers, there are also drivers for providers. This is why there have been so many new providers popping up every day. They see the benefits that can be obtained by offering cloud services.

Economies of Scale

Cloud providers make use of a concept called *economies of scale*, which is based on the fact that once you build the infrastructure for an application or service, adding capacity will only require incremental additions. What this means is that the larger the environment, the greater the potential return on investment (ROI).

For example, let's take a look at mail services. Implementing mail services internally for 5,000 employees may cost you around 25 cents per mailbox. A cloud provider implementing mail services for 100,000 users may cost the provider 10 cents per mailbox. The provider can then offer the service for 15 cents per mailbox. It's a situation where everyone wins. The provider makes money, but the cost is still cheaper than what it would be for an individual organization.

Recurring Revenue

Offering subscription-based services can provide a service provider with a recurring revenue stream. Recurring revenue adds stability to a business. A predictable revenue streams helps in revenue estimating and budgeting.

CLOUD ADOPTION INHIBITORS: WHAT IS HOLDING PEOPLE BACK?

The cloud has a number of benefits, but nothing is perfect. There are also some issues that have slowed cloud adoption. In this section we cover some of the more prevalent ones.

Ambiguity

One of the most pressing issues that have kept people from moving to the cloud is a lack of understanding of what the cloud is and what it offers. This lack of understanding causes fear. Usually the fear is around potential hidden costs, lack of control, integration issues, and security concerns. However, all the issues can be mitigated if you have a good understanding of what to look for in a cloud provider and what to expect from one. This is what we're going to help with. We're going to give you the knowledge you need to overcome the fear.

Many of the concerns are really just questions that don't have a definitive answer. When you're dealing with your organization's ability to perform its business functions, you have to be wary of the unknown. You don't want to take risks that you cannot mitigate. If you don't know what the risks are, then you certainly can't mitigate them.

Concerns Over Maturity

There are often concerns regarding the maturity of the cloud and the various cloud providers. Many newer public service providers simply do not meet the needs of many organizations. Not only do public service providers need to offer services that customers want, but they also need to offer the right levels of service and support for those services.

Services aren't Robust Enough Yet

Many of the services offered by cloud service providers are not robust enough to meet customer needs. Many public cloud services can be very specific. The provider may only offer a very niche service. If your organization isn't in need of a specific service presented in a specific way, you might not be able to take advantage of the service. As the cloud matures, so do its service offerings. Providers are continually adding and updating services to meet customer needs.

SLAs

Many service providers are not at the point where they can offer truly substantive SLAs. Some providers don't offer SLAs at all. Others offer SLAs, but the service guarantees they make are not suitable for many organizations. Your organization may need 24/7 availability for a particular service or application, but there might not be a provider that can offer that. One thing to remember is that if your organization cannot provide a certain level of availability because of a technical limitation, a service provider may face the same technical limitation for the given service or application.

Integration

When dealing with public service providers, integration is a key component. Since you will not own the systems used by the service providers, you probably won't have direct access to them. Without direct access, some sort of interfaces must be provided to allow for integration with your other systems. You may need both data integration and application integration.

Data Integration

Integrating data and reporting between on-premises and cloud-based systems can be costly. You will have to figure out a means of copying large amounts of data from one location to the other. The bandwidth used during the copy process will almost certainly affect the cost you pay for the service.

Lack of real-time data availability can present an issue in many circumstances. Real-time data is often needed for reporting. Moving data in real time can use a lot of bandwidth. This bandwidth usage can be very costly.

Application/Service Integration

Sometimes the Web interface offered by service providers is not good enough on its own. You may have a Web service or application that needs to take advantage of the provider's service. Many service providers offer interfaces or APIs that can be used to access functionality. Secure access to these interfaces allows you to access the functionality you need programmatically.

Security

Even though some people consider cloud implementations to be more secure in certain aspects than traditional deployments, other aspects are often considered less secure and more of a risk. The risk mainly comes from the fact that you will not have direct control over the systems and the data. You have to trust what the service provider is doing.

Ownership of Data

There are many questions when it comes to data ownership in the cloud. One big question with cloud implementations is, Who owns the data? Your company may have created the data, but now is it being stored at an external service provider. Do you still own it?

What happens if the service provider goes out of business? How do you get access to your data? Does the company that takes over ownership of the systems then own your data? Is that company obligated to give it to you? What happens if there is a dispute and you don't pay your bill? Can your data be held hostage? These are questions that you must ask when you're considering a service provider. Different service providers will give different answers, so you must be aware of what you can expect from your provider.

Auditing

The ability to do proper auditing can vary among cloud environments. Depending on the implementation, you may or may not have direct access to the systems or applications you want to audit. The service provider may be able to provide you access to the desired log via some application interface or by exporting the logs and sending them directly to you.

Privacy, Legal, and Compliance Issues

Privacy is a big concern when it comes to cloud implementation. The cloud provider will have direct access to your organization's data. If this data is meant to be private, you have to worry about what measures are being taken to keep it private. In certain situations, you may be violating privacy standards simply by storing the data with an external provider.

Legal and compliance issues can get very complicated when you're dealing with cloud implementations. Jurisdiction hasn't really been defined yet. If you are located in the United States and accessing servers in Europe, which regulations apply? In general, the guidance is to make sure you adhere to laws in both jurisdictions.

One method you can use to ensure that the provider has adhered to the appropriate regulations is to choose a provider that has passed a SAS70 Type II audit. This audit ensures that a provider meets a given set of compliance criteria. The audits are performed by an independent consulting agency in order to maintain integrity.

Multitenancy

Multitenancy can present its own issues. You have to be careful when you have different organizations using the same systems. There will undoubtedly be security issues and issues with customization.

Security

With multitenancy, you have very little control over or even knowledge of who may be sharing the same systems as you. You may unknowingly have competitors using those same systems. If your competitors were able to exploit some security flaw on the host system, they might be able to access your environment. The same thing goes for hackers. Hackers buy cloud space too. Their main goal may be to find and exploit areas that they can use to gain access to other environments on the same host.

Lack of Customization

When you share systems and applications with other organizations, there is a limit to the amount of customization that may be done. In some cases, you may not be able to do the customization without affecting other organizations. In other cases, the service provider may not be willing to support a customized application. You have to remember that the service provider may have thousands of customers. Supporting customization for each of those customers may be prohibitively costly.

For these same reasons, you also might not be able to stay on a certain version of an application for as long as you like. You may be forced to take new versions of the application as they are released. These new versions may require additional training. This could affect your company's productivity.

Technology Challenges

Although there have been great advancements in cloud technologies, there is still a lot of room for growth. Many technologies have not yet been officially ratified as standards. This can lead to compatibility issues. Authentication is a good example. Although standard authentication protocols have been created, they are not widely used.

Scale Out

Cloud environments generally use commodity equipment for their infrastructure. In many cases this means that to add capacity, you need to scale out instead of scaling up. Scaling out can cause increased burden on a datacenter and increased environment-related costs in resources such as power and cooling.

Corporate Policies

If your organization has used only internal solutions before, your policies and procedures may need to be updated to take cloud environments into consideration. You must develop policies that can be applied when you have complete control over the environment and when you don't. You will need policies to determine what can be moved to the cloud and what can't. You will also need policies around what will be required from service providers.

Flexibility

Choosing a cloud environment can be somewhat limiting. You have to consider how hard it would be to change providers if you are unsatisfied with one. It may be very hard to move from one provider to another. A big concern is how hard it would be to move your data to another provider if you needed to. In some cases, this may be so costly it's impossible to do.

SUMMARY

There are five key cloud characteristics: on-demand self-service, broad network access, resource pooling, rapid elasticity, and measured service. A solution must exhibit these five characteristics to be considered a true cloud solution. There are four cloud deployment models: public, private, community, and hybrid. Each deployment model is defined according to where the infrastructure for the environment is located. There are three main cloud service models: Software as a Service, Platform as a Service, and Infrastructure as a Service. SaaS was the original cloud service model but the cloud has continued to grow and expand. Now a vast array of service models is available.

There are many factors pushing organizations toward the cloud, as well as many factors that are keeping organizations away. Each organization must evaluate cloud offerings for itself to see what best fits its needs.

Laying the Groundwork

INTRODUCTION

The cloud is about services, but there are a number of technology components that come together to make it possible. These technologies and technology advances are responsible for the rapid growth of the cloud and the availability of cloud applications.

We won't get into too much depth in discussing the technologies, but it's important that you have a general understanding of them. When you have to make decisions about which cloud providers and cloud products you want to consume, it's beneficial if you can distinguish between these technologies and what they offer.

AUTHENTICATION

Authentication is the process of verifying that users are who they say they are. Before you can access resources on most systems, you have to first authenticate yourself. Anytime sensitive information is involved or anytime auditing needs to be performed, you have to make sure the person performing an action is who they say they are. If you don't, you can't really trust that person or the information they provide. Many different methods can be used to authenticate someone or something. It's important that you pick the right authentication method for a given situation.

Authentication is an important part of any environment. The cloud is no exception. In fact, in some aspects, authentication is even more important in a public cloud environment than in a traditional environment. Authentication is the primary method for restricting access to applications and data. Since public cloud applications are available via the Web, they can theoretically be accessed by anyone. For this reason, service providers need to ensure that they take the appropriate precautions to protect applications and user data. This process begins with ensuring that the appropriate authentication methods are in place.

Similarly, when you evaluate cloud providers, you need to ensure that they have the appropriate authentication measures in place. The information is this section will help you make that determination. We start by going over some general background information on authentication and authorization; then we move on to identity providers and federated authentication.

Identification vs. Verification

When you look at the issue of authentication, you can break it down into two components: identification and verification. *Identification* is the process of you stating who you are. This statement could be in the form of a username, an email address, or some other method that identifies you. Basically, you are saying, "I am drountree" or "I am derrick@gmail.com," and "I want access to the resources that are available to me."

But how does the system know that you really are drountree? The system can't just give access to anyone who claims to be drountree. This is where verification comes in. *Verification* is the process that a system goes through to check that you are indeed who you say you are. This is what most people think of when they think of authentication. They don't realize that the first part of the process is that you first have to make a statement about who you are. Verification can be performed in many ways. You supply a password or a personal information number (PIN) or use some type of biometric identifier.

Think about it this way: You know that when you attempt to authenticate to a system and you enter your username and password, the system will check to see if the combination is right. You must have entered the correct password that corresponds to the username you entered. If one or the other is wrong, the authentication attempt fails. The system will first check to see that the username you entered is a valid username. If it isn't, then an error message will immediately be returned. If is the username is valid, then system checks the password. A correct combination of the username and password is needed for successful authentication.

Authorization

After users have been authenticated, authorization begins. *Authorization* is the process of specifying what a user is allowed to do. Authorization is not just about systems and system access. Authorization is any right or ability a user has anywhere.

Every organization should have a security policy that specifies who is allowed to access which resources and what they are allowed to do with these resources. Authorization policies can be affected by anything from privacy concerns to regulatory compliance. It's important that the systems you have in place are able to enforce the authorization policy of your organization; this includes public cloud-based systems.

Advanced Authentication Methods

In securing your data applications, simple username and password authentication may not be sufficient. You should take extra care in situations where the identity of the person making a request may be especially questioned, such as external requests to internal systems. Public cloud systems can also present a heightened risk. Since your public cloud applications and data are freely available over the Internet, you might want to look to a provider that offers advanced authentication methods to secure them. Let's look at two commonly used methods: multifactor authentication and risk-based authentication.

Multifactor Authentication

One method for ensuring proper authentication security is the use of *multifactor authentication*. Multifactor authentication gets its name from the use of multiple authentication factors. You can think of a *factor* as a category of authentication. There are three authentication factors that can be used: something you know, something you have, and something you are. *Something you know* would be a password, a birthday, or some other personal information. *Something you have* would be a one-time use token, a smartcard, or some other artifact that you might have in your physical possession. *Something you are* would be your biometric identity, like a fingerprint or a speech pattern. In order for something be considered multifactor authentication, it must make use of at least two of the three factors mentioned. For example, when a user attempts to authenticate, he or she may have to enter both their password and a one-time use token code.

Multifactor authentication is being offered by an increasing number of service providers, especially those that store sensitive data. Often this advanced functionality is not advertised prominently by cloud providers. So, if you feel that multifactor authentication is necessary in your deployment, you should ask the provider about it.

Risk-Based Authentication

Risk-based authentication has just started to gain popularity. Risk-based authentication actually came about because of the increased risk facing public applications and Web sites. Risk-based authentication uses a risk profile to determine whether the authentication request could be suspect. Each authentication attempt is given a risk score. If the risk score exceeds a certain value, the Web site or service provider can request additional information before allowing access. This additional information could be in the form of security questions or an additional authentication factor.

A risk is calculated based on user and system characteristics. The site will create a profile for each user based on information such as usual login time, system used to access the site, or access method. When a user attempts to access the site and their current usage characteristics do not match their profile, their current risk score would reflect the variation.

Risk-based authentication has become very popular for banking and financial sites. But, like multifactor authentication, risk-based authentication may not be advertised, so you should ask the cloud provider if they can supply it.

Identity Providers

In the authentication arena, there is a particular service provider called an identity provider. An *identity provider*, or IdP, is an entity that holds identity information. You can have an IdP set up internally, or you can use a service provider. Users, also called *entities*, authenticate against the IdP's credential store. The IdP then allows access to the user's identity information. It's important to note that an IdP does more than just authenticate a user. It holds the user's identity information. Upon authentication, this information can be sent to whomever needs it. Generally, this will be a service provider, also referred to as the *relying party*. This is because the service providers rely on the IdP for authentication and identity information.

Credential Store

The *credential store*, sometimes called the *user store* or the *authentication store*, is where the actual user credentials are stored. Two main types of authentication stores are being used with IdPs today: databases and directory stores. In general, with databases, credentials are stored in proprietary tables created by the user management application. One of the reasons databases are often chosen as credential stores is because a majority of developers have experience coding against a database, so it's relatively easy for them to write code to authenticate users. Directory stores include Lightweight Directory Access Protocol (LDAP) stores and Active Directory (AD) implementations. LDAP provides a simple standards-based approach to accessing information from the credential store. Active Directory is Microsoft's domain-based approach to LDAP. Using an AD credential store generally requires that you use proprietary access methods. Many cloud service providers are now offering the option to use your internal credential store instead of their third-party store. This way, users don't have to remember multiple sets of credentials.

To help you understand the concept a little better, refer to Figures 2.1 and 2.2. Figure 2.1 shows a traditional authentication architecture where the applications interface directly with the authentication store. Figure 2.2 shows how it works with an IdP. The applications interface with the IdP, and the IdP interfaces with the credential store.

FIGURE 2.1
Traditional Authentication Architecture

  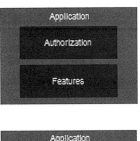 

FIGURE 2.2
Federated Authentication Architecture

Public IdPs

Identity providers can be public or private. The use of public IdPs is steadily increasing. Instead of creating internal IdPs, many organizations have decided to use an IdP service provider. Using an external IdP can save you a lot time and money when it comes user management. There are several public IdPs available for use. We'll cover a few of the most popular.

FIGURE 2.3

OpenID Logo

OpenID

We'll start with OpenID. OpenID is not an identity in and of itself; it is a standard for doing authentication. It provides an open framework that providers can use to ensure interoperability of their solutions. OpenID is a technology that allows you to implement an environment where authentication is abstracted from authorization. With OpenID, authentication can be decoupled from an application or other resource. You can use a central entity, such as an IdP, to perform authentication for multiple Websites and resources. As long as the IdP adheres to the OpenID standard and the service provider supports it, the interoperability will work properly.

OpenID provides several key benefits. First, service providers do not have to worry about maintaining authentication capabilities. They do not have to build authentication support into their services or applications. They also do not have to worry about maintaining credential stores or doing user management. Password resets and things of that nature that quickly drive up support costs are eliminated.

Second, with OpenID, the service provider does not care what method was used to authenticate the user. This allows you to select an authentication scheme that meets your organization's needs without having to worry about whether or not it will work with your applications. You can also feel free to change your authentication scheme when you deem it necessary. It can be a change within the same IdP, or you can choose a new IdP. As long as the IdP supports OpenID, your application will not care that the authentication mechanism has changed. If you did choose a new IdP, you will have to set up a new trust between the application or service and the IdP, but it will not affect authorization within the application or service. This type of flexibility can be a big advantage in today's ever-changing landscape.

Google

Google based its IdP on the OpenID standard. It conforms to OpenID 2.0. The Google IdP also supports the following extensions: OpenID Attribute Exchange 1.0, OpenID User Interface 1.0, OpenID+OAuth Hybrid Protocol, and Provider Authentication Policy Extension (PAPE). When you use your Google account to log onto sites like YouTube, you are actually using the Google IdP.

Facebook

Facebook is rapidly growing in popularity as an identity provider. Facebook currently uses OAuth 2.0 to provide authentication and authorization.

Facebook offers several APIs and software development kits (SDKs) that aid you in integrating Facebook login with your application. You can use client-side JavaScript, native device calls (iOS, Android, etc.), or server-side execution. Go to www.facebook.com/developers to get more information on using the Facebook identity provider.

Microsoft Account

Microsoft's identity provider, Microsoft account, was previously known as Windows Live. It's the default IdP used on all Microsoft-related Websites. It is also the default IdP for Microsoft Access Control Services (ACS), Microsoft's federated identity provider service, which we discuss next.

Federated Identity

Federated identity is a secure way for disparate systems to get access to your identity information. Your information may only exist in one system. But, with federated identity, other systems can also have access this information. The key to federated identity is trust. The system that holds your information and the system that is requesting your information must trust each other. To make sure your information is being transmitted to a trusted place, the system that holds the information must trust the system that is requesting the information. The system requesting the information has to trust the sender to ensure they are getting accurate and trustworthy information.

Basically, an application is trusting another entity, namely an IdP, when that entity says who a particular user is. The application does not itself perform any actions to verify the user's identity. It simply believes what the IdP says. Before an application will believe an IdP, a trust relationship must be established. The application must be configured with the address of the IdP that it will be trusting. The IdP must be configured with the address of the application. In most cases, some type of keys will be exchanged between the two entities to actually establish the relationship. These keys are used by the entities to identify themselves with the other entities.

Microsoft Access Control Services

You can choose to go with an externally hosted issuer like Microsoft Access Control Service (ACS). ACS is a Windows Azure cloud-based Web service used for identity and access management. ACS can be used to provide authentication and authorization functionality for Web applications and services. This way, those functions don't have to be built directly into the code for the application or service. A key benefit of ACS is that because it is a cloud-based instance, no installation is required. You still have to configure the instance for your environment, but nothing needs to be installed.

ACS is very extensible. It complies with a large number of environments and protocols. This allows you to easily integrate ACS into your environment. ACS supports industry-standard protocols such as OAuth, OpenID, WS-Federation, and WS-Trust. ACS also supports multiple token formats. It supports SAML 1.2, SAML 2.0, JWT, and SWT formats. ACS supports development using a variety of Web platforms. You can use .NET, PHP, Java, Python, and a host of others.

ACS includes a host of functionalities that are critical for most federated identity environments. ACS allows you to implement only the functionality you need for your implementation. ACS provides the following functionality: authentication, authorization, federation, security token flow and transformation, trust management, administration, and automation.

COMPUTING CONCEPTS

A couple of key computing concepts come into play when you're talking about cloud implementations. These concepts help establish many people's philosophy of cloud implementations.

Utility Computing

The concept of utility computing has been around for a very long time, but it's just now being put into practice. *Utility computing* is the practice of treating computing resources like a metered service, as we do for electricity and water. A utility company only charges you for the electricity or water you use. It's the same in utility computing. The service provider only charges you for the computing resources you use.

This concept of pay-as-you-go computing is at the center of the public cloud methodology. There are resources available to you, but you should only pay for what you use. Often there is also a monthly fee associated with having the resources available, but the bulk of the cost is based on your actual usage.

Commodity Servers

The concept of commodity servers involves using general, nonspecialized servers to complete a task. Instead of using different servers for different tasks, you use the same servers for all tasks. Generally, commodity servers are lower-cost systems. Instead of putting many tasks on one powerful server, you can spread the task over a larger number of less powerful servers. This practice is also referred to as *scaling out* instead of scaling up.

Cloud providers often use commodity servers for building out their virtualization infrastructure. This is what Amazon did for its cloud implementation. In fact, Amazon has been so successful that other providers have since tried to copy this model.

Autonomic Computing

Autonomic computing, proposed by Paul Horn of IBM in 2001, shared the vision of making all computing systems manage themselves automatically. It refers to self-managing characteristics of distributed computing resources, which recognize and understand changes in the system, take appropriate corrective actions completely automatically, with close to zero human intervention. The key benefit is drastic reduction in the intrinsic complexity of computing systems and making computing more intuitive and easy to use by operators and users. The vision is to make computing systems self-configuring, self-optimizing, and self-protecting—as well as self-healing.

Independently, several similar efforts arose toward simplified IT management, such as ITIL (IT Infrastructure library) methodologies and ITSM (IT service management) technologies, WSDM (Web Services distributed management), and the like. Several research groups are still working on self-healing systems and policy management systems that can handle sophisticated service-level agreements to enable better automated decision making. We have seen some good success with many products now also focusing on easy manageability as one of the important goals.

Given that the objective of cloud computing is to simplify computing systems and provide elasticity in computing and high availability of systems, any new innovation toward making machines more autonomic will directly feed into cloud infrastructures. Virtualization technologies … provide the right level of abstractions to dynamically handle changes to the hardware resources and cater to on-demand elasticity. … It may not be wrong to say that cloud computing shares the vision of autonomic computing and more.

Application Service Providers

The trend of hosting applications as a service for others to use started as early as the 1990s. The vendors who would host such applications accessible by their clients using just Web browsers were called *application service providers*. With this definition, it does look very similar to SaaS, and SaaS vendors could be called ASPs. However, there were several limitations when any off-the-shelf application with a browser-based interface was hosted as a service.[1] Many of these applications did not have the capability to handle multitenancy, customized usage for every user, and did not have automated deployment and elasticity to scale on demand. Nevertheless, it is safe to say that the ASP model was probably a forerunner of the SaaS model of cloud computing.

[1] *Differences between ASP model and SaaS model. www.luitinfotech.com/kc/saas-aspdifference.pdf [accessed 13.10.11].*

HARDWARE VIRTUALIZATION

When many people think about the cloud, they automatically think virtualization. But in fact virtualization is not required in building a cloud environment. If you think back to the characteristics of a cloud environment, none of them specially mentions virtualization as a requirement.

Although it's not required, virtualization is used in a majority of cloud implementations. This is because virtualization can increase your ability to deliver the characteristics required in a cloud environment. For example, it can be much cheaper to increase capacity by adding a new virtual machine than it would be to provide this increase using physical systems.

Hardware virtualization is the most common and most well known type of virtualization. Hardware virtualization is used to generate a simulated physical system on top of an actual physical system. In most cases there are multiple simulated physical systems. This is how hardware virtualization is used to create system density and increase system utilization. You can have multiple virtual systems, called *virtual machines*, running on a single physical system. These virtual systems will share use of the physical resources. So, when one virtual system is not using a physical system's resources, the resources may be used by another physical system. In a nonvirtualized environment, system resources may be sitting idle a large portion of the time. You've paid for the system but are not using it to its full potential.

Hypervisors

Hardware virtualization is implemented through the use of *hypervisors*. Hypervisors do offer some network and storage virtualization, but robust features are added by other products. For this section, we are concerned with hardware virtualization. We cover some of the more common hypervisors used in cloud environments today. Depending on what service you will be consuming, the hypervisor may be very important in your decision. You need to make sure the hypervisor supports the features you need in your implementation.

Hypervisor Basics

The hypervisor is what actually provides the virtualization capabilities. The hypervisor acts as an intermediary between the physical system, also called the *host*, and the virtualized system, also called the *guest*. Different hypervisors require different components be installed on the host system to provide virtualization. Furthermore, different hypervisors provide different options for guest operating systems.

Hypervisor Types

There are two types of hypervisor: Type-1 and Type-2. Hypervisors are categorized based on where they sit in the stack.

Type-1 hypervisors generally sit directly on top of the bare-bones hardware. Type-1 hypervisors act as their own operating systems. This allows them to make more efficient use of physical system resources. Because of this efficiency, most cloud environments are built using Type-1 hypervisors.

Type-2 hypervisors generally sit on top of another operating system. The operating system controls access to the physical hardware. The hypervisor acts as a control system between the host operating system and the guest operating system. One of the big advantages of Type-2 hypervisors is that you can generally install them on your regular desktop system. You don't need to have a separate system for installing the hypervisor.

Xen Hypervisor

There are two versions of the Xen hypervisor: the open-source version of Xen and the commercial version offered by Citrix, called XenServer. For this book, we will be talking about XenServer.

FIGURE 2.4
Xen Hypervisor Logo

XenServer is a type-1 hypervisor; basically it is a customized version of Linux that is installed on your server hardware. A XenServer implementation consists of two main components: the XenServer hypervisor, which is installed on a bare-metal system, and the XenCenter management console, which is installed on a Windows system.

Hyper-V

Hyper-V is a type-1 hypervisor. Many people are often fooled by it. Hyper-V is enabled after the Windows operating system is installed, and Hyper-v-based virtual machines are accessed through the Windows operation system. But the fact is, when you enable Hyper-v, it inserts itself between the hardware and the operating system. As a matter of fact, the operating system you see is essentially a virtual machine running on the Hyper-v platform.

vSphere

VMWare offers a type-1 hypervisor call vSphere. VMWare vSphere is widely used within organizations to provide a virtualization infrastructure and private cloud functionality. But it's use in public cloud infrastructures has been somewhat hindered because of its proprietary nature.

FIGURE 2.5
xSphere Hypervisor Logo

KVM

The Kernel-based Virtual Machine, more commonly known as KVM, is an open-source Linux kernel-based hypervisor. KVM uses a loadable kernable module named kvm.ko and a platform-specific model, either kvm-intel.ko or kvm-amd.ko. KVM supports a wide variety of Windows and Linux operating systems for the guest operating system (OS).

FIGURE 2.6
KVM Hypervisor Logo

WEB DEVELOPMENT TECHNOLOGIES

Web applications are accessed via the Internet, typically using a Web browser. Web applications generally don't require any other client installations. This is one of the things that make them particularly attractive in cloud-based scenarios. They can be accessed from anywhere and in many cases from any device, as long as the device has a suitable Web browser.

More and more independent software vendors (ISVs) are offering Web-based versions of their applications. In fact, Web apps are becoming the *de facto* standard for offering applications. Several standards and technologies go into making Web applications a viable solution. We cover a few of them here.

In addition, it's very important to consider Web application technologies in assessing PaaS platforms. Since you will be using the PaaS platform to develop applications, it's important that you ensure that the PaaS platform you choose supports the technologies that you plan to use to implement your applications.

HTML

HyperText Markup Language (HTML) has been a Web standard for a very long time. In fact, HTML is the number-one standard for creating Web pages. All Web browsers know and understand how to interpret HTML pages. HTML uses tags to format and add structure to Web pages. The number of tags and amount of functionality available in HTML continues to expand. In fact, the newest version HTML 5 has again made HTML a choice Web programming language.

FIGURE 2.7
Adobe Flash Logo

Adobe Flash

Adobe Flash is a programming language used mainly for creating vector graphics and animation. Flash is probably one of the most common languages used on the Internet for applications that need animation.

Flash isn't as popular as it once was due to concerns over stability and security. Because of these issues, some systems do not support Flash natively. Developers have been looking for alternatives that can provide the same functionality. HTML 5 is one of the technologies that many see as a potential replacement for Flash.

SOAP

SOAP, the Simple Object Access Protocol, is a protocol for exchanging data between Web services. SOAP messages use XML Information Set for their formatting. SOAP relies on other protocols for its negotiation and transmission. The two most common application layer protocols SOAP uses are HTTP and SMTP. The three characteristics of SOAP that make it an attractive protocol are its neutrality, its independence, and its extensibility.

REST

REST, or Representational State Transfer, is actually an application architecture. REST breaks down application interactions into servers and client. The client is the entity making the request, and the server is the entity servicing the request.

REST defines six constraints on application implementations:

- *Client/server model.* There must be a strict separation of concerns between clients and servers.
- *Stateless.* Applications must not rely on state information when interfacing with clients.
- *Cacheable.* The content received by clients must be cacheable.
- *Layered system.* Clients cannot tell whether or not they are directly connected to servers; therefore intermediaries can be used when needed.
- *Code on demand.* Servers can send executable code to clients.
- *Uniform interface.* A standard interface is used between clients and servers.

Java

Java is an object-oriented programming language. Java applications are designed to run on any platform. Java code is interpreted to an intermediate language called *Java bytecode*. This bytecode is then run by the Java Virtual Machine (JVM). As long as a system has the correct version of the JVM running, the Java application should be able to run.

JavaScript

JavaScript (JS) is a lightweight, object-oriented programming language. All current Web browser versions understand JavaScript. Sometimes you will see that for security reasons, the execution of client-side JavaScript has been disabled. JavaScript was initially used as mainly a client-side language, but nowadays it is used increasingly for both client- and server-side programming. Because of the wide compatibility of JavaScript, it is used in a large number of Web site and Web application implementations.

FIGURE 2.8
Java Logo

ASP.NET

ASP.NET is a server-side Web development language developed by Microsoft. It allows a developer to build dynamic pages called *Web forms*. This means that the content on the page can change based on certain characteristics or requirements. ASP.NET is built on top of Microsoft's Common Language Runtime (CLR). The CLR does just-in-time compilation of applications written using any programming language based on Microsoft's .NET Framework.

FIGURE 2.9
Microsoft .NET Logo

PHP

PHP is a server-side scripting and programming language. PHP used to stand for Personal Home Page; now it stands for PHP: Hypertext Preprocessor. Many server-side programming languages require a Web page to call a separate file, but PHP code can be embedded directly in a Web page.

FIGURE 2.10
PHP Logo

FIGURE 2.11
Ruby on Rails Logo

Ruby on Rails

Ruby on Rails, also called Ruby, is an open-source development framework that can be used to create templates, develop applications, and query databases. Ruby uses the Model-View-Controller, or M-V-C, architecture. A model maps to a table in a database. A View is an ERB file that is converted to HTML at runtime. A Controller is the component that responds to external requests.

JBOSS

JavaBeans Open Source Software Application Server (JBOSS) is an open-source application server. It is used to implement the Java Platform, Enterprise Edition (JSEE). JBOSS is written in Java, which means it can be run on systems that support Java applications.

FIGURE 2.12
JBOSS Logo

JSON

JavaScript Object Notation (JSON) is an open standard used to represent arrays and data structures. JSON is largely used to transmit data between a server and a Web application. As the name indicates, JSON is derived from JavaScript, but it's important to note that even though it's derived from JavaScript, JSON is language independent. This is one of the characteristics of JSON that makes it attractive to developers.

FIGURE 2.13
JSON Logo

SUMMARY

In some cases, you will need only minimal understanding of the technologies behind the cloud. In others, you will need a much greater understanding. It's important that you understand which technologies are in play when you're making decisions about cloud providers. If you need to integrate with a cloud implementation, it's vital that you understand with which technologies you are integrating. These could be authentication technologies, computing technologies, virtualization technologies, or Web development technologies.

Cloud Deployment Models

INTRODUCTION

NIST defines four cloud deployment models: public clouds, private clouds, community clouds, and hybrid clouds. A cloud deployment model is defined according to where the infrastructure for the deployment resides and who has control over that infrastructure. Deciding which deployment model you will go with is one of the most important cloud deployment decisions you will make.

Each cloud deployment model satisfies different organizational needs, so it's important that you choose a model that will satisfy the needs of your organization. Perhaps even more important is the fact that each cloud deployment model has a different value proposition and different costs associated with it. Therefore, in many cases, your choice of a cloud deployment model may simply come down to money. In any case, to be able to make an informed decision, you need to be aware of the characteristics of each environment.

PUBLIC CLOUDS

Public clouds are environments that are entirely managed and serviced by an external service provider. When most people think about computer clouds, it is public clouds they are thinking about. In fact, most of the articles and material you find regarding clouds are in fact referring to public clouds. This is because

35

the first cloud environments were public clouds. The idea of there being other types of cloud deployments took a little while to develop. Public clouds are still the most deployed cloud environments.

Benefits

The number of public cloud implementations continues to grow at a rapid pace due to the numerous benefits public clouds offer. The value proposition for a public offering is very strong, although there are some drawbacks, as we shall see.

Availability

Public cloud deployments can offer increased availability over what is achievable internally. Every organization has an availability quotient that they would like to achieve. Every organization also has an availability quotient that they are capable of achieving. Sometimes the two match; sometimes they don't. The problem is that availability comes at a cost, whether hardware cost, software cost, training cost, or staffing cost. Whichever it is, an organization may not be able to afford it, so they have to make do with what they have and therefore not be able to achieve the level of availability they would like.

Most public cloud providers already have the hardware, software, and staffing in place to make their offerings highly available. They may charge a little extra for the service to provide increased availability, but it will be nowhere near the cost of doing it internally. However, just because you go with a public cloud provider, you should not assume high availability or fault tolerance. You need to ask the provider what is offered with the service. If increased availability is an add-on, you need to know that when you calculate the cost. You should also ensure that the availability you desire is part of your service-level agreement (SLA). Your SLA can give you a level of assurance that your availability needs will be met.

Be aware that although public clouds can increase your availability, you have to make sure you are cognizant of what will be available. It will depend on the service offering. In a SaaS offering, the application itself will be available. But if it's a PaaS or IaaS offering, although the platform or infrastructure may be available, the application might not be. Application issues will not be mitigated by using a public IaaS or PaaS offering.

Scalability

Public cloud implementations offer a highly scalable architecture, as do most cloud implementations. What public cloud implementations offer that private clouds do not is the ability to scale your organization's capacity without having to build out your own infrastructure.

Public cloud implementations can offer temporary burst capacity or permanent capacity, depending on which your organization needs. If your organization is using a SaaS service, you can add users to the application without
adding the associated infrastructure. If you are using an IaaS or PaaS service, you will have increased capacity to build applications and services, but
you will still need to ensure that the application you built can handle the
increased load.

Accessibility

Public cloud providers place great importance on accessibility. To expand their
potential customer base as wide as possible, they attempt to ensure that they
can service as many different client types as possible. Their goal is to ensure
that their services can be accessed by any device on the Internet without the
need for VPNs or any special client software.

Nowadays people access the Internet and Internet-based applications using
more than just traditional browsers on traditional laptops and desktop computers. People are choosing to use an abundance of new Web browsers. Tablets
and smartphones have also gained widespread use. Although the new devices
have Web browsers, they are not fully featured Web browsers. So, to be able
to support these devices, Web pages and Web applications must be somewhat
simplified and must adhere to interoperable development standards.

It can be very expensive supporting multiple operating systems and multiple Web browsers. The development and quality assurance (QA) costs can be
extremely high. So, even though many organizations want to provide this type
of support to users, it might be cost prohibitive. However, since service providers are more focused on offering a single set of services, they are more amena-
ble to accepting these costs.

Cost Savings

Public clouds are particularly attractive because of the cost savings they offer.
But you do have to be careful because the savings might not be as good as
you think. You need to have a good understanding of not only the *amount* of
savings but also the *type* of savings.

Public clouds offer the most savings in terms of upfront costs. Using a cloud,
organizations don't have to worry about spending money for initial hardware
and software deployments. The service provider pays for these costs. The customer only has to pay for the services used. Most of these upfront costs would
be capital costs because of the hardware that would need to be purchased.

There are also support and maintenance savings that would be incurred—not
just from hardware and software and support and maintenance but also from
environment costs. Since the servers will not be in your datacenter, you will

save on space, electricity, and cooling costs. In fact, if you outsource all your applications, you might not need your own datacenter at all. These are the cost savings that are really driving organizations to the cloud. The fact of the matter is that few organizations will be able to outsource all their IT activities, however, at least in the near term.

Drawbacks

Public cloud implementations do have their own set of limitations and drawbacks. A lot of these can be traced back to the fact that the infrastructure is actually owned and controlled by another organization. So, one of the big drivers of public clouds is also one of the biggest inhibitors.

Integration Limitations

In public SaaS clouds, the systems are external to your organization; this means that the data is also external. Having your data housed externally can cause problems when you're doing reporting or trying to move to on-premises systems. If you need to run reports or do business intelligence (BI) analytics against the data, you could end up having to transmit the data through the Internet. This can raise performance concerns as well as security issues. Reports render much more quickly when they are generated in the same location as the data.

Application integration can also be a problem in public SaaS offerings. In an ideal situation, different applications can use shared functionality. You don't want to repeat functionality in two different applications. So if the functionality exists in one application, you want another application to be able to call the functionality in another application. This can be a problem in public cloud applications. The application provider must expose APIs or web services that a customer can use in order to make this happen. If not, you may end up in a situation where functionality it repeated.

Reduced Flexibility

When you are using a public cloud provider, you are subject to that provider's upgrade schedule. In most cases, you will have little or no influence over when upgrades are performed. Even if it is possible for you to run a different instance than other customers, many providers are reluctant to deploy multiple versions of an application or system online. Doing so would increase their administrative overhead. Users will have to be trained on the new system, which may have an impact on productivity.

Forced Downtime

When you use a public cloud provider, the provider controls when systems are taken offline for maintenance. Maintenance may be performed at a time that is inconvenient for you and your organization. Depending on how the system is partitioned, you may be able to postpone maintenance for a short period of time and agree on a time that is convenient for both your organization and the provider. However, it is highly unlikely that maintenance can be postponed for a long period of time.

Responsibilities

With public clouds, most of the responsibilities lie with the service provider. The provider is responsible for maintenance and support. The provider is also responsible for making sure support personnel are properly trained. This is a very attractive proposition for customer organizations with limited staff.

In a public cloud, the service provider is responsible for all the components needed to implement the service. These components vary depending on the service offered. They can include servers, storage, applications, and data.

In a public cloud, the customer is responsible for everything needed to consume the service. There are some exceptions, such as implementations in which a client-side application is involved. The customer is responsible for installing the client-side application and ensuring that it is functioning properly. The service provider is responsible for developing the client-side application and offering support to get it working properly.

The customer is responsible for general client maintenance. The customer must ensure that the necessary updates and patches have been installed on the client systems. The customer is also responsible for providing network connectivity to the provider. The provider will be publicly accessible, but the customer must ensure that the clients have a route or path to the provider.

Security Considerations

Ensuring security is especially difficult in public cloud scenarios. Since you probably won't manage access to the systems providing the services, it's very difficult to ensure that they are secure. You basically have to take the provider's word for it and trust in the provider's capabilities.

Data

Public cloud providers raise a real issue over data security. There is a question of data ownership. Since the service provider owns the systems where your data resides, the provider could potentially be considered the true owner of the data.

There is also an issue with data access. Theoretically, anyone who works at the service provider could potentially have access to your data.

Compliance

Compliance can be a big concern with public service providers, much to do with the fact that you will have little to no visibility around what's happening on the back end. For most things, you will have to take the provider's word that the provider is compliant. The provider may have a SAS-70 certificate, but without being able to examine it for yourself, you have to trust that the SAS audit was performed sufficiently.

Auditing

In the case of public cloud providers, you will generally have limited auditing capabilities. You may not direct access to any logs or event management systems. You will most likely not be able to implement any back-end alerting or logging of your own. So you will have to rely on what the provider supplies. Many public cloud providers will allow you access to at least some form of application logs. These logs can be used to view user access and make decisions regarding licensing.

PRIVATE CLOUDS

Private clouds are completely managed and maintained by your organization. Generally all the infrastructure for the environment will be housed in a datacenter that you control. So, you are responsible for purchase, maintenance, and support.

Many people have an understanding of the cloud such that they do not believe that private clouds are actually clouds. They feel only public clouds are true clouds. But if you look at the characteristics of clouds, you can see that it doesn't matter where the cloud is hosted. The value proposition of the cloud changes when you talk about private clouds as opposed to public clouds; but the value proposition doesn't determine whether it's a cloud a not.

Benefits

There are many benefits to going with a private cloud model. Most of these benefits center around your ability to monitor and control what goes on in the cloud environment.

Support and Troubleshooting

Private cloud environments can be easier to troubleshoot than public cloud environments. In a private cloud environment, you will have direct access to all systems. You can access logs, run network traces, run debug traces, or do anything else you need to do to troubleshoot an issue. You don't have to rely on a service provider for help.

If you are doing your own support and troubleshooting, you theoretically can provide much faster turnaround times, which will help maintain customer satisfaction. In the end, customer satisfaction is paramount to maintaining the success of your environment.

Maintenance

With private clouds, you control the upgrade cycle. You aren't forced to upgrade when you don't want. You don't have to perform upgrades unless the newer version has some feature or functionality that you want to take advantage of. You can control when upgrades are performed. If your organization has regularly scheduled maintenance windows, you can perform your upgrades and other maintenance activities during that specified timeframe. This may help reduce the overall impact of a system outage.

In some instances, you might need to run multiple versions of an application. This could be for compatibility, for example. If you do not control the systems, you might not be able to access multiple versions of the application. With an internal cloud, you are free to run multiple versions of an application when needed. This flexibility gives you an increased ability to service your customers' needs.

Monitoring

Since you will have direct access to the systems in your private cloud environment, you will be able to do whatever monitoring you require. You can monitor everything from the application to the system hardware. One big advantage of this capability is that you can take preemptive measures to prevent an outage, so you are able to be more proactive in servicing your customers.

Drawbacks

Although having control over the environment provides you with many benefits in a cloud environment, it also presents you with issues. When you implement a private cloud, you will run into some of the same drawbacks you would see implementing a traditional internal solution. You have to weigh these issues against the benefits to find out if an internal cloud is the right environment for you.

Cost

Implementing a private cloud requires substantial upfront costs. You have to implement an infrastructure that not only can support your current needs but your future needs as well. You need to estimate the needs of all the business units you will be supporting. You also have to implement an infrastructure that can support peak times. All the systems needed to support peak times don't always have to be running if you have a way of automatically starting them when necessary.

Hardware and Software Compatibility

You have to make sure the software you implement is compatible with the hardware in your environment. In addition, you have to make sure the software you implement is compatible with the clients in your environment. There may be instances where you need specialized hardware—storage, for example—to implement a particular application.

Expertise Needed

With private clouds you still need expertise in all the applications and system you want to deploy. The need for internal expertise can lead to expensive training and education. You will be responsible for installing, maintaining, and supporting them, so you must ensure that you either have the in-house knowledge to do so or the ability to bring in outside contractors or consultants to help.

Building a cloud environment requires staff with knowledge of hardware, storage, networking, security, and virtualization. It can be very difficult to find employees who have all of this knowledge. In addition, your organization will need someone who has expertise in the particular cloud platform you want to implement.

Responsibilities

In a private cloud environment, the division of responsibilities is pretty straightforward. Your organization will be responsible for the end-to-end solution. You are responsible for the systems that provide the service, the client applications, and the maintenance of the client systems.

Security Considerations

With a private cloud implementation, your organization will have complete control over the systems, applications, and data. You can control who has access to what. Ensuring security is easier in a private cloud environment. There you have complete control over the systems, so you can implement any security means you like.

In a private cloud environment, you will be able perform your security and compliance audits. This will give you greater confidence, knowing that your systems are meeting your security and compliance needs.

Compliance

In a private cloud environment, you are responsible for making sure that you follow any applicable compliance regulations. If your organization has the skills and the technology to ensure adherence to compliance regulations, having the systems and the data internal can be a big advantage. If you don't have the skills and technology, you will have to obtain the skills, or you could face serious problems.

Having your systems and data housed at an external facility can aid your company with compliance. You can rely on the external provider to provide the skills and expertise needed. Payment card industry (PCI) compliance is a good example. PCI compliance requires special considerations to be taken for any system that processes credit card information. One thing you can do is outsource credit card processing to a third party. This can help ease some of the requirements on some of your internal systems.

You have to be careful, however. You can't rely completely on the cloud provider. If there are security or compliance issues, your company can still be sued or at least suffer damage to your reputation. Many people won't make a distinction between your company and the provider. Others will blame you for choosing a bad provider.

Data
In a private cloud environment, you own the data and the systems that house the data. This gives you more control over who can access the data and what they can do with it. It also gives you greater assurance that your data is safe.

Auditing
In a private cloud environment, you have complete access to all the application and system logs. You can see who accessed what and what they did with it. The biggest advantage is that you can see all of this in real time, so you are able to take any corrective action necessary to ensure the integrity of your systems.

COMMUNITY CLOUDS

Community clouds aren't used as much as public or private clouds; in fact, they are the least known and least used cloud deployment model. In a community cloud, the cloud is shared by a group of organizations that have a common purpose or goal. The cloud environment is generally built to help them achieve that purpose or goal.

Benefits
There are many benefits to having a community cloud. A lot of them center around the fact that the infrastructure, and hence the cost, is shared.

Cost
In a community cloud, costs are shared between the community members. This shared cost allows for the purchase of infrastructure that any single member organization may not have been able to afford. This way the community members are also able to achieve greater economies of scale. But you have to be careful, because issues may arise around who is responsible for which costs. There could

also be issues around who actually "owns" which components of the infrastructure. These aspects must be clearly defined at the start of the initiative.

Multitenancy

In a community cloud, multitenancy can help you take advantage of some economies of scale. Your organization alone may not be large enough to take advantage of some of the cost savings, but working with another organization or multiple organizations, together you may be large enough to see these benefits.

In a community cloud, multitenancy also allows you to share support and maintenance activities. Instead of one organization needing to have all the skills to support and maintain the environment, each organization can contribute in the areas where it has expertise.

Drawbacks

There are some potential drawbacks to implementing a community cloud. Any time you have multiple organizations working together, there is the potential for conflict. Steps must be taken to mitigate any potential issues.

Ownership

Ownership in a community cloud needs to be clearly defined. If multiple organizations are coming together to assemble infrastructure, you must determine some agreement for joint ownership. If you are purchasing capital resources, those resources need to go against some organization's budget. In some instances, the organizations coming together to build the community cloud may establish a single common organization that can "own" the resources.

Responsibilities

In a community cloud, responsibilities are shared between the member organizations. There may be problems deciding who owns what and who is responsible for what, but after those questions have been decided, the shared responsibility can be quite beneficial. This shared responsibility reduces the administrative burden on any single organization.

Security Considerations

Community clouds present a special set of circumstances when it comes to security because there will be multiple organizations accessing and controlling the environment.

Data

In a community cloud, all the participants in the community may have access to the data. For this reason, you don't want to store any data that is restricted to only your organization. You could be setting yourself up for a big headache if you do.

Compliance

In a community cloud, compliance can be particularly tricky. The systems will be subject to all the compliance regulations to which each of the member organizations is subject. So, your organization may be subject to regulations with which you have little familiarity.

Auditing

In a community cloud, member organizations will have shared access to all the application and system audit logs. You will want to have some agreement as to who will perform what activities. Trolling though logs can be particularly tedious and time consuming, so you don't want people wasting time doing duplicate work.

HYBRID CLOUDS

As the cloud computing era matures, *hybrid clouds* will most likely become the most common cloud implementation. There is a slight misconception about what a hybrid cloud actually is. Many people think a hybrid cloud is a cloud environment in which some components are public and some are private. This is not that case. A hybrid cloud environment, as seen in Figure 3.1, is one in which multiple separate clouds environments are connected together.

Hybrid clouds can offer the best of both worlds as well as the worst of both worlds. Hybrid clouds offer the freedom to implement whatever is necessary to meet your organization's needs, but hybrid clouds can also be complex and expensive to implement.

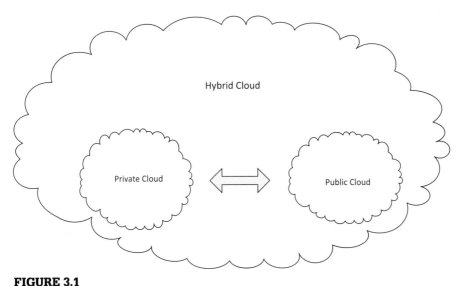

FIGURE 3.1
Hybrid Cloud Environment

Benefits

In addition to the benefits brought by each of the cloud models, the hybrid cloud model brings increased flexibility. If your ultimate goal is to move everything to a public service provider, a hybrid environment allows you to move to a cloud environment without being forced to move everything public until the time is right. You may have certain applications for which the public service offerings are very expensive. You can keep these applications internal until the price comes down. You may also have security concerns about moving certain types of data to a public service provider. Again, the hybrid cloud model allows you to leave that data internal until you can be assured that it will be safe in a public cloud environment.

Many organizations use a hybrid cloud model to provide fault tolerance and high availability. You can have certain applications hosted in two environments. That way, if one environment goes down, you can still access the application.

Drawbacks

A hybrid cloud environment can be the most complex environment to implement. You have different considerations for each type of cloud you plan to implement. Not all your rules and procedures will apply to all environments. You will have to develop a different set of rules and procedures for each environment.

Integration

You may have some applications in a private cloud and some applications in a private one, but these applications may need to access and use the same data. You have two choices here: You can duplicate copies of data, which would require you to set up some type of replication mechanism to keep the data in sync, or you can move data around as needed. Moving data around in a hybrid cloud environment can be tricky because you have to worry about bandwidth constraints.

Security Considerations

Hybrid clouds can bring about particular security considerations. Not only do you have to worry about security issues in each individual environment, you have to worry about issues created by connecting the environments together.

Data

Moving data back and forth between cloud environments can be very risky. You have to ensure that all environments involved have satisfactorily secured data. Data in motion can be particularly difficult to secure. Both sides of the conversation must support the same security protocols, and they must be compatible with each other.

Auditing

Auditing in hybrid environments can be tricky. User access may rotate between internal and external. Following a process from start to finish may take you through both internal and external systems. It's important that you have some way of doing event log correlation so that you can match up these internal and external events.

SUMMARY

NIST has outlined four cloud deployment models: public, private, community, and hybrid. Public clouds are open to the general public. Private clouds are specific to a particular organization. Community clouds are shared by multiple organizations. Hybrid clouds are environments made up of a combination of cloud models. Each model has its set of benefits, drawbacks, and security implications.

CHAPTER 4

Cloud Service Models

CHAPTER POINTS

- Software as a Service
- Platform as a Service
- Infrastructure as a Service
- Additional Service Models

INTRODUCTION

According to the National Institute of Standards and Technology (NIST) definition of cloud, there are three main cloud service models: Software as a Service (SaaS), Platform as a Service (PaaS), and Infrastructure as a Service (IaaS). These are the three original cloud service models. But one thing to remember is that since we are dealing with service providers, almost everything is negotiable. Existing services are changed and new services are added to meet customer needs. As the cloud market grows, we have to acknowledge the existence of many other service models today. We cover a few of the more prevalent ones in this chapter.

Each service model has its own set of characteristics and criteria. Figure 4.1 provides a simple overview of today's computer-related services. As we go through each of the cloud service models, we'll look at how they break down again the entire stack.

SOFTWARE AS A SERVICE

Many people consider SaaS the original cloud service model. A SaaS model is similar to the old application service provider (ASP) model. There are some key differences. First, in the older ASP model, the applications hosted were usually client/server applications. Some types of special infrastructure and client were usually needed to access the applications. However, most of today's SaaS

| Users | |
| Client Systems | |

Network Connectivity

Applications	
Infrastructure Software	
Operating System	
Virtualization Layer	
Physical Servers	
Networking and Storage	
Mechanical and Electrical	

FIGURE 4.1
Computer-Related Services
Stack

applications are Web-based applications that do not require any special clients. This simplifies the process needed to access the applications. Furthermore, in the ASP model, customers generally accessed different instances of an application. In SaaS, customers generally access the same application; there are simply different partitions or views of the application.

SaaS Characteristics

Now let's get into some of the characteristics of typical SaaS deployments. Depending on the service provider and the service being offered, the characteristics may differ slightly, but here we cover the most common scenarios.

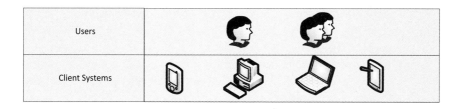

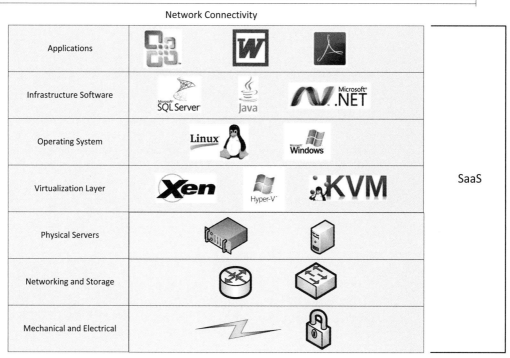

FIGURE 4.2
SaaS Services

Figure 4.2 outlines the services you can typically expect from a SaaS provider.

Customization

With SaaS implementations, the service provider usually controls virtually everything about the application. In many cases, this will limit any customization that can be done. But depending on the implementation, you may be able to request that the user interface (UI) or the look and feel of the application be modified slightly. Usually wholesale changes are not allowed. In most cases the customer will not be to make the changes themselves; the provider will have to make the changes.

In a SaaS environment, allowing customization can be very costly for the service provider and, hence, the customer. Allowing extensive customization may mean hosting a separate instance of an application just for a particular customer. Having extensive customization can also cause a problem when it comes time do a software upgrade. It's highly probable that the customization would be lost when the upgrade occurs. Then it would have to be recreated by either the customer or the provider. This may require a large amount of time; and time is money.

Support and Maintenance

In a SaaS environment, software upgrades are centralized and performed by the service provider. You don't have to worry about upgrading software on multiple clients. The centralized upgrades allow for more frequent upgrades, which can allow for accelerated feature delivery. The exception to this rule is when there is client software that is used to access the centralized application. But must SaaS providers will try to provide access to their applications without requiring a client application.

Centralized upgrades can present a problem. When the provider decides it's time to upgrade, you have little to no choice in the matter. First, if there is downtime associated with the upgrade, you will simply have to accept it. In addition, the upgrade may require additional user training, so you will have to train your users on the new software. This can lead to downtime or, at the very least, periods of decreased productivity.

Analytics

Analytics and usage statistics can provide value information about application usage. In SaaS implementations, the provider has the ability to view user activities and determine trends. In many cases this information is shared with the customers. For large organizations, this information can be invaluable. Since most cloud environments are pay-as-you-go offerings, it's important to understand usage trends. Understanding trends helps you understand when you may have a spike in usage and therefore a spike in costs. It's also important to understand concurrent usage and total usage. You may be able to reduce your license costs.

Integration

In a SaaS environment, the data will be stored at the provider site. In most cases, the customer will not have direct access to the data. This can be a problem when it comes to reporting and business intelligence. It's also a problem if you need to do a manual fix of the data or load or reload data in bulk. In some cases there is nothing you can do about that.

In some implementations you may be allowed to move data back and forth between the SaaS instance and your local in-house systems. You have to be careful with the amount of bandwidth used during these types of operations.

Not only may you incur charges from the SaaS provider, but you may also incur charges from your Internet provider.

Responsibilities

In SaaS implementations, most of the responsibilities fall on the service provider. This is one of the reasons SaaS implementations have become so popular. Organizations are able to free up their internal resources for other activities, as opposed to using them for system administration. Figure 4.3 gives you an idea of what is generally the responsibility of the service provider and what is usually taken care of by the customer.

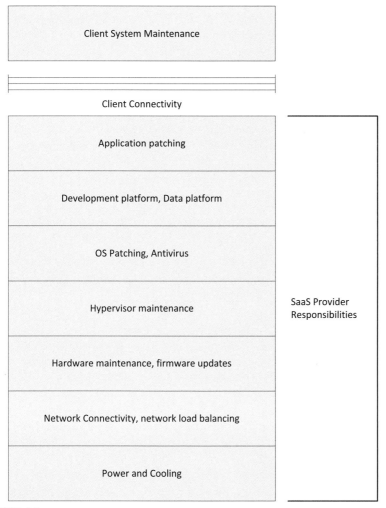

FIGURE 4.3
SaaS Responsibilities

In a SaaS environment, the provider is basically responsible for everything except the client systems. It will ensure that the application is up to date. It will make sure that the systems have been patched appropriately. It will ensure that the data is being stored properly. It will monitor the systems for performance and make any adjustments that need to be made.

In a SaaS environment, the customer is responsible for the client system or systems. The customer must ensure that the clients have connectivity to the SaaS application. The client systems must have any necessary client software installed. The client systems must be patched to an appropriate level.

SaaS Drivers

Many drivers have contributed to the rise of public SaaS offerings. There has been a big rise in the creation and consumption of Web-based applications. Users are getting used to the look and feel of these types of applications. Not to mention the fact that the look and feel have improved. Most SaaS providers offer their services in the form of Web-based applications. So, as acceptance of Web-based applications grows, so does the acceptance of SaaS services.

Not only have the look and feel of Web-based applications improved, but so have the quality and ease with which they can be developed. The maturity of older platforms and protocols and the introduction of new ones have created a wide variety of tools that can be used for creating robust Web applications. Some of these tools are HTML5, JavaScript, CSS, Ruby on Rails, and PHP.

SaaS Challenges

Even though SaaS is currently the most popular cloud service model, there are still many challenges to the adoption of SaaS. SaaS providers have been able to resolve many of the challenges and mitigate concerns, but many still exist, as described in the following sections.

Disparate Location

SaaS applications are generally hosted offsite. This means connections between the client and the application must travel over the public Internet, sometimes long distances. This distance may introduce latency into the environment. This can be a limiting factor for some applications. Some applications require response times in milliseconds. These applications will not work in environments where there is a great deal of latency.

Multitenancy

Multitenancy can cause several issues. Since the application is shared, generally little to no customization can be performed. This can be a problem if your organization requires extensive customization. You may have to go with an on-premises application.

Multitenancy also presents security issues. Since customers will generally be accessing the same instance of an application, an application flaw may allow one customer access to another customer's data. SaaS providers must be vigilant about fixing applications when they are detected. The longer an issue goes unresolved, the riskier it is for customers.

Other Security Challenges

One of the big worries organizations have with SaaS is around the security of the data. The employees at the service provider will have direct access to the systems that house the data. One way to mitigate this is to protect the data at the software level. You would have to encrypt the data at rest and the data in motion. This would prevent the provider from reading the data when it's stored or the provider's systems and when it's traveling on the provider network.

SaaS Providers

There are a multitude of public SaaS providers out there. Here we cover a few of the most popular.

Outlook.com

Web-based email is one of the most popular SaaS offering. Different providers have been offering Web-based email for a long time. Most providers offer a free service and a paid service. Outlook.com, shown in Figure 4.4, is Microsoft's mail service. Outlook.com is the successor of Hotmail and Live Mail.

A default Outlook.com mail account is free. If you want advanced features or a version that does not include advertisements, you have to upgrade your account. This can be done by selecting the gear icon in the top-right corner and selecting More Mail Settings. The Inbox Option page, shown in Figure 4.5, will appear. Here you will have an option to Upgrade to Ad-free Outlook. This will take you to the Microsoft Website, where you can purchase access to the upgraded version of the application.

Google Drive

Google Drive, shown in Figure 4.6, gives you online access to view and create word processing documents, spreadsheets, presentations, and a host of other documents.

You can use the built-in document types or add new types. To add a new type of document, choose Create in the left pane and select Connect More Apps. This will bring up the Connect Apps window shown in Figure 4.7.

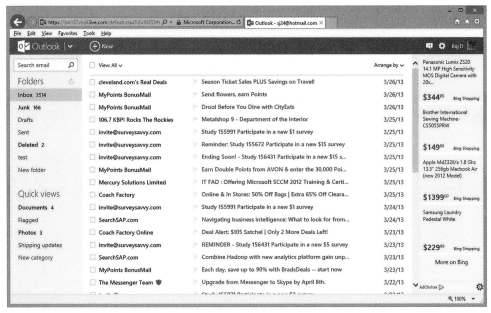

FIGURE 4.4
Outlook Mail

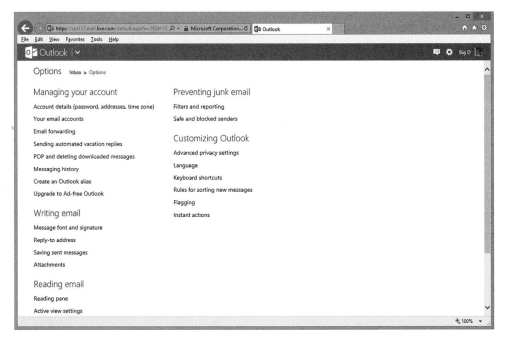

FIGURE 4.5
Outlook Mail Inbox Options

FIGURE 4.6
Google Docs

FIGURE 4.7
Connect Apps Window

Salesforce.com

Salesforce.com [1] is a well-known customer relationship management (CRM) application used for financial, delivery, and staffing related to business systems operations. A CRM application consists of a set of workflows (business processes) together with software that helps manage customer-related activities and information. These activities could be related to sales (such as using customer information to generate future leads), marketing tasks (like using historical sales data to develop sales strategies), or providing better customer service (by using call center data). Salesforce.com provides a comprehensive list of features for all three of these types of activities. This section, however, focuses on the features of Salesforce.com for customer support representatives as a case study of SaaS usage.

A Feature Walk-Through

Before a business can start using Salesforce.com, there is a small setup phase where the business user can customize Salesforce.com for their business requirements. This involves first obtaining a Salesforce.com account. Second, the system administrator belonging to the business has to import their existing customer data into Salesforce.com, customize the various Salesforce.com screens, and give access rights for the appropriate screens to the employees of the business. The following description does not go into the details of this setup and assumes that the required configuration has already been set up.

After the Salesforce.com portal has been set up, customer support representatives can log in and go to the `Call Center` Web page, shown in Figure E4.1. This page contains functionality for handling customer requests, such as recording customer calls, assigning the cases to support personnel, and searching for solutions. The Web page contains a number of tabs. Figure E4.1 shows the `Cases` tab, which helps support representatives to keep track of and handle customer complaints. It can be seen that the Web page allows us to search for a particular case, look at recent cases, and generate useful reports such as the total number of cases. The tool `Mass Email` allows us to send an email to the email ID associated with each case. The default fields for a case can be seen by clicking on the `Create New` bar to the left

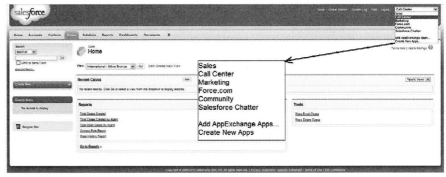

FIGURE E4.1

Salesforce.com.

---

[1] *SalesForce.com. http://www.salesforce.com [accessed October 2011].*

of the Web page. This brings up the screen shown in Figure E4.2, which can be used by support (call center) personnel who are generating a new case from a phone call. The `Contact Name` and `Account Name` fields can be found by searching the `Contacts and Accounts` database. Many of the fields, for example, `Priority` and `Case Origin`, are values selected from a pull-down menu. In Salesforce.com, this is referred to as a *picklist*. Additional fields can be added to the case record by the administrator, thus customizing this page to the needs of each enterprise.

NOTE

To test the functionality presented here, readers can visit www.salesforce.com and sign up for a free account.

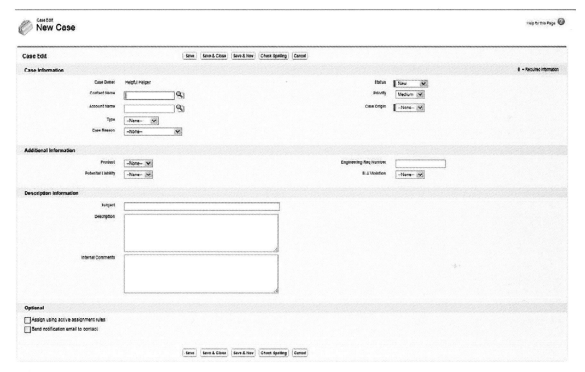

FIGURE E4.2
Salesforce.com: New Case screen.

The other tabs on the page contain some interesting functionality that is useful for employees handling customer calls. For example, the `Solutions` tab provides access to a database containing earlier solutions to customer problems. This database is searchable, allowing employees to quickly resolve customer problems. The full list of tabs can be found by clicking on the "+" sign. The administrator can customize the tabs visible on each screen. The `Sales` and `Marketing` Web pages contain functions useful for sales and marketing, respectively, and are similar to the `Call Center` page. Furthermore, the `Community` and `Salesforce Chatter` Web pages allow for instant messaging, forums, and other types of collaboration between users. It can be seen that the application interface is designed to suit a typical business need and hence can be customized to reuse as an application for a new business.

The `Add App Exchange App` tab (Figure E4.4) enables users to extend the functionality of Salesforce.com by installing applications from the Salesforce.com. AppExchange portal and the `Create New App` tab allow users to create new applications (over Salesforce.com) and offer them for free download or purchase through AppExchange. Access to these tabs can be controlled by the administrator for the enterprise. Advanced features of the platform can be accessed using the Force.com link, a complete featured platform on which Salesforce.com executes, as described in the next section.

Once a new case has been created, it is possible to click on the case ID to get the details of the case. The page also contains a button to create an activity associated with the case, which could be a task or an event (such as a meeting to discuss the case). Figure E4.3 shows the screen for creating a new task. This screen contains fields for assigning a task to another agent, setting a deadline, and so on.

It is not always necessary to manually enter cases. Salesforce.com has features to automatically create cases from the Web as well as custom emails. For creating cases automatically from a self-service Web page, the administrator can create a Web script using the Salesforce.com application that can be included in the Website belonging to the business. Salesforce.com has other advanced features for assisting customer support representatives. For example, cases can also be automatically generated by extracting fields from customer emails. There are also features to support softphones, case teams consisting of employees with different roles, and creating case hierarchies. Details of these advanced features are beyond the scope of this book but can be found under the link `Cases` in the Help page.[2]

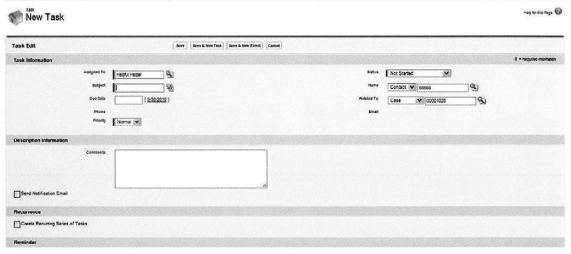

FIGURE E4.3
Salesforce.com new task screen.

[2] https://na3.salesforce.com/help/doc/user_ed.jsp?loc=help [accessed March 2011].

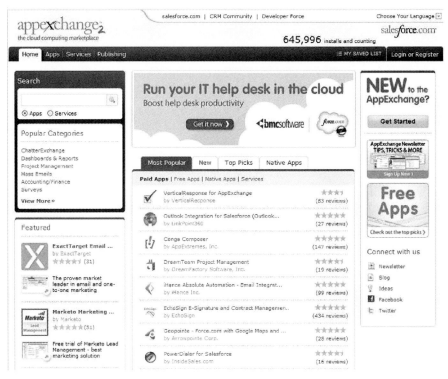

FIGURE E4.4
Salesforce.com AppExchange.

Customizing Salesforce.com
So far we have described the standard features and Web pages on Salesforce.com. However, businesses will want to customize Salesforce.com to suit their business processes. This is a very important aspect of supporting *multitenancy* in a SaaS application. A brief overview of some important customizations and details are presented next.

> **NOTE**
>
> **Customizing the application**
> - Change field names
> - Set conditions for field updates
> - Set conditions for email alerts
> - Customize the UI

As stated earlier, Salesforce.com allows businesses to rename fields of all Salesforce.com database objects, as well as adding custom fields. For example, businesses can add fields to the case record shown in Figure E4.2 to keep track of data unique to the business. Fields like the `Product` field, which are selected via a picklist, can be set to product codes for the business. Workflows (business processes) are captured in Salesforce.com by means of a series of rules. For example, *assignment rules* shown in Figure E4.2 can be used to automatically assign cases to support representatives. By updating assignment rules, customer case workflow can be tailored to business needs. Apart from task rules, other types of rules that can be implemented are (i) email alerts, which send an email alert under certain condition (e.g., confirmation of a sale), (ii) field updates (e.g., when a contract is about to expire), and (iii) outbound messages that interface to an external system (e.g., send a message to a finance system when an invoice is approved). Details can be found on the portal describing the creation of a Workflow Rules Website.[3]

Finally, both administrators and users can customize the look and feel of the user interface. This includes items such as the placement and content of text and graphics, names and numbers of tabs on each screen, and the overall layout of the screen. Administrators can set an overall look and feel for the business and give employees rights to personalize their individual views. More details of this aspect can be found under the Customize link on the Help page.[2]

Another SaaS application with functionality similar to that of Salesforce.com is Sugar CRM,[4] which is an Open Source CRM suite. A comparison of Sugar CRM and Salesforce.com by the Salesforce. com team appears in.[5]

---

[3] *Creating Workflow Rules. https://login.salesforce.com/help/doc/en/creating_workflow_rules.htm [accessed October 2011].*
[4] *SugarCRM. http://www.sugarcrm.com/crm/ [accessed October 2011].*
[5] *White Paper.http://www.salesforce.com/ap/form/sem/why_salesforce:ondemand. jsp?d=70130000000EN1GandDCMP=KNC-Googleandkeyword=sugar%20 CRMandadused=1574542173andgclid=CNfqoLK2uaQCFc5R6wod_R3TbQ [accessed March 2011].*

PLATFORM AS A SERVICE

PaaS is service offering whereby customers are given a platform to use for their computing needs. In most instances, this platform is used for development. Depending on the provider, the development platform could be simply an operating system or a full development platform that includes a Web server and development libraries.

Figure 4.8 outlines the services you can typically expect from a PaaS provider.

PaaS Characteristics

PaaS implementations allow organizations to build and deploy Web applications without having to build their own infrastructure. PaaS offerings generally include facilities for development, integration, and testing. Here we cover some of the characteristics generally seen in PaaS environments.

As we go through these characteristics, we need to be mindful of what happens in PaaS environments. When an organization moves to a PaaS implementation, it will implement some type of application or service on the platform. The provider generally has no control over how the application or service is developed or over the quality of development. In many deployments, the

Platform as a Service

Users	
Client Systems	

Network Connectivity

Applications	
Infrastructure Software	SQL Server · Java · Microsoft .NET
Operating System	Linux · Windows
Virtualization Layer	Xen · Hyper-V · KVM
Physical Servers	
Networking and Storage	
Mechanical and Electrical	

PaaS

FIGURE 4.8
PaaS Services

provider will offer additional services, such as basic load-balancing services, to help with your deployment.

Customization

With PaaS, you have complete control over the application, so you are free to customize the application as you see fit. You won't be able to make many changes to the development platform, however. In most cases, this platform will be strictly controlled by the provider. There will likely be different configuration options that you can set, but true customization will be limited.

Analytics

Since you, the customer, will be creating the applications, you will have the ability to view application usage and determine trends. You will be able to see which components are getting the most use and which ones are not being used.

In a PaaS environment, you will also usually have visibility into the use of the platform. You will be able to determine when new systems need to be added to handle the load. Often, providers give you the ability to automatically spin up new systems when your current ones meet certain load thresholds.

Integration

In a PaaS environment, the data will be stored at the provider site, but the customer will have direct access to it. Conducting business intelligence and reporting should not be a problem from an access point of view, but you could run into issues when it comes to bandwidth usage, because you may be moving large amounts of data between your internal environment and the provider's environment. So there might be performance concerns there, as opposed to access or functionality concerns.

PaaS Responsibilities

In a PaaS offering, responsibilities are somewhat distributed between the service provider and the customer (see Figure 4.9).

The provider will take care of everything at the development platform level and below. The provider will make sure the operating system is patched and up to date when it's delivered to you. The provider will also do periodic operating system updates that will be rolled out to you.

In a PaaS implementation, the customer is generally responsible for everything above the operating system and development platform level. You will be responsible for installing and maintaining any additional applications you will need. This includes application patching and application monitoring. The database platform may be supplied for you, but you will be responsible for the data. In a PaaS implementation, you will usually have direct access to the data. If there are any problems with the data, you will be able to implement any direct data fix you might need to perform.

PaaS Drivers

There have been many drivers influencing the growth of the PaaS market. Many organizations want to move towards a public cloud model, but can't find public SaaS providers offering the applications they need. A PaaS model allows them to move the infrastructure and platforms out of their internal datacenters while allowing them to be able to develop the applications they need.

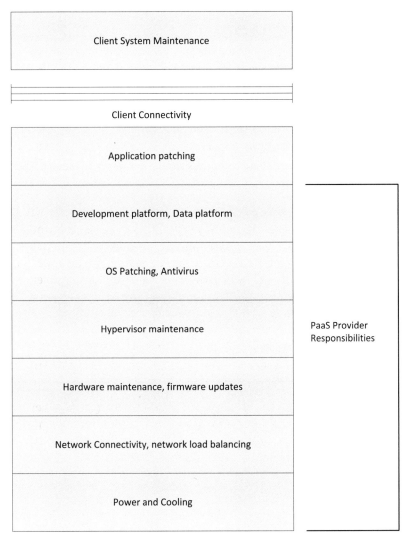

FIGURE 4.9
PaaS Responsibilities

PaaS Challenges
A number of challenges come into play with public PaaS environments, including issues related to flexibility and security.

Flexibility Challenges
You may have difficulty finding a provider with the platform you need. Most PaaS providers limit their offerings to specific platform sets. If you need a

special set or special configuration, you might not be able to find a provider that offers what you need.

Security Challenges

The provider will have administrative control over the operating system and the database platform. Since the provider has direct access to the systems, they will have direct access to all of the applications and data.

PaaS Providers

The number of PaaS providers in the market continues to grow. First we take a look at Windows Azure.

Windows Azure

Windows Azure, shown in Figure 4.10, was one of the first PaaS offerings to hit the market. Windows Azure has a free offering and upgraded offerings that include features such as increased SLAs. Windows Azure makes it very easy to spin up a Web site or development platform. Windows Azure includes a wide variety of options such as compute services, data services, app services, and network service.

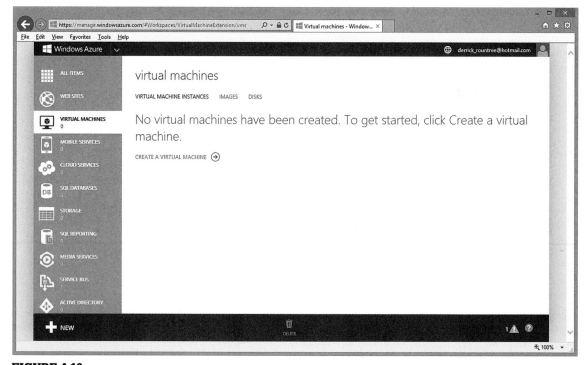

FIGURE 4.10
Windows Azure

Google App Engine

Google App Engine is a PaaS solution that enables users to host their own applications on the same or similar infrastructure as Google Docs, Google Maps, and other popular Google services. Just as Microsoft Azure provides a platform to build and execute .NET applications, Google App Engine enables users to develop and host applications written using Java, Python, and a new language called Go.[6] The platform also supports other languages that use Java Virtual Machine (JVM) runtime, such as JRuby, JavaScript (Rhino), and Scala programming languages.

The applications hosted on Google App Engine can scale both in compute and storage, just like other Google products. The platform provides distributed storage with replication and load balancing of client requests. The applications can be easily built using the Eclipse Integrated Development environment with which many developers are familiar. This section gives a simple overview and key highlights of the platform.

Getting Started

Step-by-step instructions for using Google App Engine are described here, based on the procedure available as of the writing of this book.[7] The developer first signs up for a Google App Engine account using his or her Gmail credentials. Figure E4.5 shows the first screen when the application is being configured.

Google App Engine allows a newly developed application to be served from the developer's own domain name. For example, if the developer chooses myapp as an application name, the application will be served at http://myapp.appspot.com. This URL can be shared publicly or selectively shared with a small group of members. Every developer can host up to 10 applications for free, with 500 MB of complimentary storage. The developer needs to pay a nominal amount for the storage and bandwidth resources used by the application beyond these limits. A simple dashboard showing the usage metrics for each application can be seen on the portal, a screenshot of which is shown in Figure E4.6.

NOTE

Developing and Deploying on Google App Engine
1. Download the SDK (Eclipse plug-in).
2. Create a new "Web Application Project."
3. Configure the application.
4. Develop code.
5. Test in simulated App Engine environment.
6. Deploy to Google App Engine.

Developing a Google App Engine Application

To develop Java applications, the App Engine software development kit (SDK) needs to be installed. The SDK is an Eclipse plug-in (Figure E4.7) that includes build, test, and deployment environments and is available at http://dl.google.com.eclipse/plugin/3.x. To get started, create a new project as a Web Application Project; right-click the project name and select **Google** in the preferences and enter a valid application ID for the project. After developing (programming) the application, during

---

[6] http://golang.org/doc/go_tutorial.html. [accessed June 2011].
[7] http://code.google.com/appengine/. [accessed June 2011].

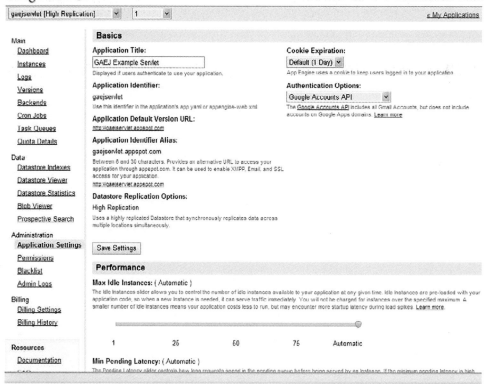

FIGURE E4.5

Google App Engine: Application configuration.

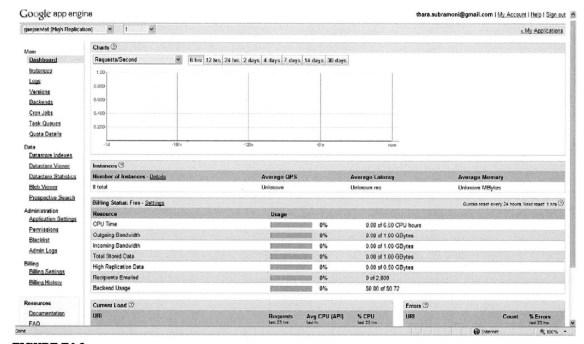

FIGURE E4.6

Application dashboard of Google App Engine.

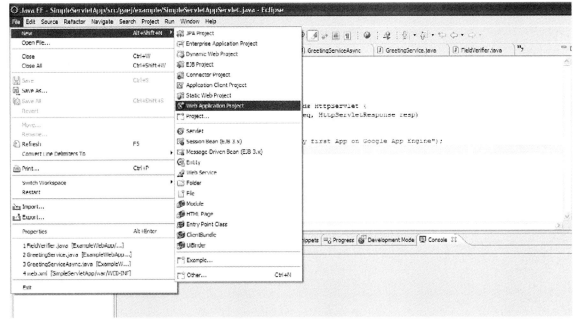

FIGURE E4.7
Google App Engine Eclipse plug-in.

the deployment stage we need to specify an app ID for the application. To deploy onto the App Engine, similar to creating the application, simply right-click on the project name and select the **Deploy to App Engine** option, and the application will be uploaded onto the App Engine and will be deployed.

Another interesting option during application configuration is an option to create a Google Web Toolkit (GWT) application. GWT basically allows us to create interactive applications with drag-and-drop facility to author a custom graphical interface. The toolkit then automatically converts the UI portion into JavaScript with AJAX [8] (asynchronous) calls to access the backend logic on the server. Note that since JavaScript runs within a browser (client side) and AJAX provides a nonblocking way of accessing the back end, the overall effect is a good experience with quick response for interactive applications. A skeleton code for GWT can be created using the following command:

```
webAppCreator -out myFirstApp com.cloudbook.myFirstApp
```

The developer can also check the **Generate GWT Sample Code** option during application creation to create a default Greeting project (Figure E4.8). If this option is unchecked, we could write our own Java servlet code and deploy it on the App Engine, as discussed earlier. So, literally any Web application written in Java can be deployed on the App Engine.

---

[8] *Ajax learning guide. http://searchwindevelopment.techtarget.com/tutorial/Ajax-Learning-Guide. [accessed June 2011].*

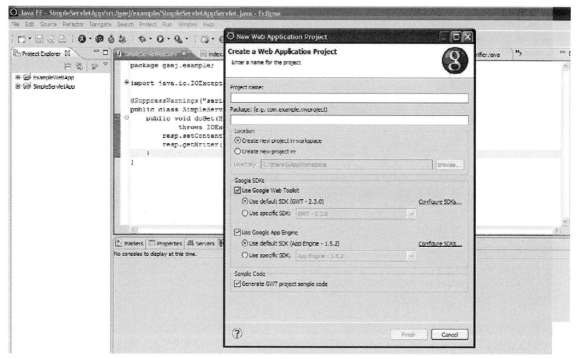

FIGURE E4.8
Google App Engine App deployment.

The SDK comes with a local Web server for test deployment. This local Web server simulates the secure runtime or App Engine sandbox environment with limited access to the underlying operating system. For example, the application can only be accessed using HTTP on specific ports. It cannot write to the file system and can read only files that were uploaded along with application code. An additional restriction with the sandbox environment is that the application, when accessed over HTTP, should return a response code within 30 seconds. These restrictions are mainly to prevent one application from interfering with another.

INFRASTRUCTURE AS A SERVICE

IaaS provides core services such as computing power, storage, networking, and operating systems. You can then build your environment on top of these resources (see Figure 4.11).

An IaaS provider may provide you with hardware resources such as servers. These servers would be housed in the provider's datacenter, but you would have direct access to them. You could then install whatever you needed to onto the servers. This can be costly, though, because the provider would not be

Users	
Client Systems	

Network Connectivity

Applications	
Infrastructure Software	
Operating System	
Virtualization Layer	
Physical Servers	
Networking and Storage	
Mechanical and Electrical	

IaaS

FIGURE 4.11
IaaS Services

able to make use of multitenancy or economies of scale. Therefore, customers would have to absorb all the costs of the systems themselves.

A more common model is for an IaaS provider to provide you with virtual machines that you can use to install whatever you need. These virtual machines could be running Windows, Linux, or some other operating system. Then you can do whatever you want on top of the operating system. Because the systems are virtualized, the provider is able to take advantage of multitenancy. These systems can host many different customers on the same set of physical hardware. They can greatly increase their density. The provider can then pass the cost savings on to you.

Responsibilities

In an IaaS deployment, the customer is responsible for most of the environment (see Figure 4.12). The provider is responsible for the hypervisor layer (if used) and below. This includes physical hardware, storage, and networking. The physical hardware will be stored in the provider's datacenter, but the customer may have full access to it.

The customer is responsible for obvious things like operating system and application maintenance. However, a few not-so-obvious things need to be considered, such as antivirus. The customer is responsible for ensuring that

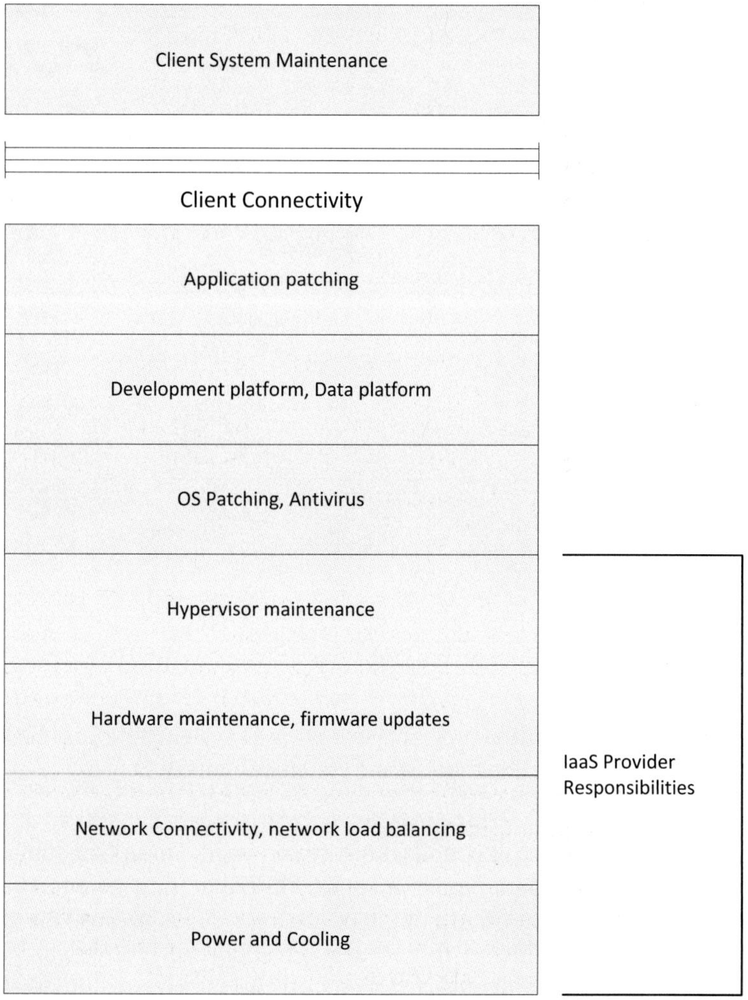

Client System Maintenance

Client Connectivity

Application patching
Development platform, Data platform
OS Patching, Antivirus
Hypervisor maintenance
Hardware maintenance, firmware updates
Network Connectivity, network load balancing
Power and Cooling

IaaS Provider Responsibilities

FIGURE 4.12
IaaS Responsibilities

systems have up-to-date antivirus. You don't want to get caught running a publicly available system without antivirus or some other type of threat protection.

Drivers

Many organizations look to IaaS providers to expand their capacity. Instead of spending a lot of money expanding a datacenter or building a new datacenter, organizations are basically renting systems provided by an IaaS provider.

Organizations are also looking at IaaS providers to provide burst capacity. Some organizations need increased capacity only on certain occasions. For this reason, they don't want to spend money on costly permanent solutions. An IaaS provider customers them to add capacity on a temporary basis. With IaaS, customers pay for the increased capacity only when they need it.

Challenges

There have been several challenges to IaaS adoption. Most organizations see the benefits, but they worry about the loss of control. The total cost can also be an issue. In many IaaS environments, you are charged for resource usage, such as processor and memory. Unless you carefully monitor your system usage, you may be in for a shock when the bill comes.

Security Challenges

The security challenges for IaaS implementations are similar to those for other service providers. However, since the provider does not need access to the actual operation system or items at a higher level, there is no need for them to have administrative accounts on the system. This can give the customer at least some level of comfort regarding security.

IaaS Providers

IaaS providers are really picking up steam in the marketplace. This isn't just due to demand. There is also the fact that IaaS platforms such as CloudStack and OpenStack have been developed to make automation and orchestration easier. Here we cover two of the most well-known IaaS providers: Amazon EC2 and Rackspace.

Amazon Elastic Compute Cloud (EC2)

The other important type of IaaS is *compute as a service*, whereby computing resources are offered as a service. Of course, for a useful compute-as-a-service offering, it should be possible to associate storage with the computing service (so that the results of the computation can be made persistent). Virtual networking is needed as well so that it is possible to communicate with the computing instance. All these together make up Infrastructure as a Service (IaaS).

Amazon's Elastic Compute Cloud (EC2), one of the popular compute-as-a-service offerings, is the topic of this section. The first part of this section provides an overview of Amazon EC2, followed by a simple example that shows how EC2 can be used to set up a simple Web server. Next, we present a more complex example that shows how EC2 can be used with Amazon's StaaS offerings to build a portal whereby customers can share books. Finally, we show an example that illustrates advanced features of EC2.

Overview of Amazon EC2

Amazon EC2 allows enterprises to define a virtual server, with virtual storage and virtual networking. The computational needs of an enterprise can vary greatly; some applications may be compute-intensive, and other applications may stress storage. Certain enterprise applications may need certain software environments; other applications may need computational clusters to run efficiently. Networking requirements may also vary greatly. This diversity in the compute hardware, with automatic maintenance and ability to handle scale, makes EC2 a unique platform.

Accessing EC2 Using AWS Console As with S3, EC2 can be accessed via the Amazon Web Services console at http://aws.amazon.com/console. Figure E4.9 shows the EC2 Console Dashboard, which can be used to create an *instance* (a compute resource), check status of user instances, and even terminate an instance. Clicking on the **Launch Instance** button takes the user to the screen shown in Figure E4.10, where a set of supported operating system images (called *Amazon Machine Images,* or AMIs) are shown to choose from. Once the image is chosen, the EC2 instance wizard pops up (Figure E4.11) to help the user set further options for the instance, such as the specific OS kernel version to use, whether to enable monitoring, and so on. Next, the user has to create at least one key-value pair that is needed to securely connect to the instance. Follow the

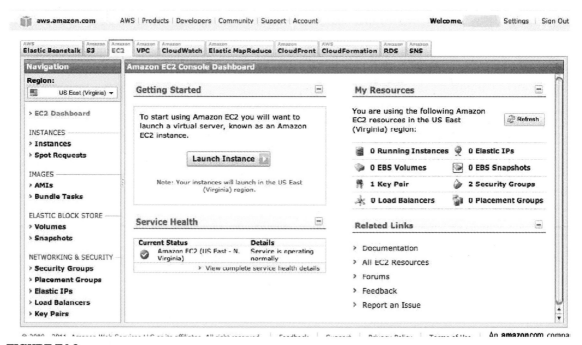

FIGURE E4.9

AWS EC2 console.

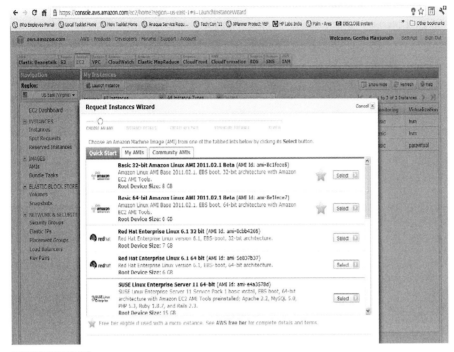

FIGURE E4.10
Creating an EC2 instance using the AWS console.

instructions to create a key pair and save the file (as, say, `my_keypair.pem`) in a safe place. The user can reuse an already created key pair in case the user has many instances (it is analogous to using the same username and password to access many machines).

Next, the security groups for the instance can be set to ensure that the required network ports are open or blocked for the instance. For example, choosing the **Web server** configuration will enable port 80 (the default HTTP port). More advanced firewall rules can be set as well. The final screen before launching the instance is shown in Figure E4.12. Launching the instance gives a public DNS name that the user can use to login remotely and to use as though the cloud server was on the same network as the client machine.

For example, to start using the machine from a Linux client, the user gives the following command from the directory where the key-pair file was saved. After a few confirmation screens, the user is logged into the machine to use any Linux command. For root access, the user needs to use the `sudo` command.

```
ssh -i my_keypair.pem ec2-67-202-62-112.compute-1.amazonaws.com
```

For Windows, the user needs to open the `my_keypair.pem` file and use the **Get Windows Password** button on the AWS Instance page. The console returns the administrator password that can be used to connect to the instance using a Remote Desktop application (usually available at **Start->All Programs -> Accessories -> Remote Desktop Connection**).

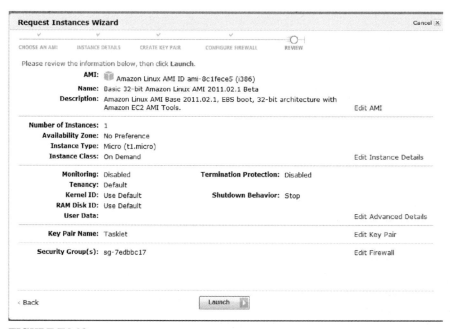

Request Instances Wizard   Cancel ☒

CHOOSE AN AMI   INSTANCE DETAILS   CREATE KEY PAIR   CONFIGURE FIREWALL   REVIEW

Number of Instances: 1

Availability Zone: No Preference

Advanced Instance Options

Here you can choose a specific kernel or RAM disk to use with your instances. You can also choose to enable CloudWatch Detailed Monitoring or enter data that will be available from your instances once they launch.

Kernel ID: [Use Default ▾]   **RAM Disk ID:** [Use Default ▾]

Monitoring: ☐ Enable CloudWatch detailed monitoring for this instance (additional charges will apply)

User Data:
○as text
○as file
☐ base64 encoded

Termination Protection: ☐ Prevention against accidental termination.

Shutdown Behavior: [Stop ▾] Choose the behavior when the instance is shutdown from within the instance.

‹ Back   [Continue ▷]

FIGURE E4.11

The EC2 instance wizard.

Request Instances Wizard   Cancel ☒

CHOOSE AN AMI   INSTANCE DETAILS   CREATE KEY PAIR   CONFIGURE FIREWALL   REVIEW

Please review the information below, then click **Launch**.

AMI: 📦 Amazon Linux AMI ID ami-8c1fece5 (i386)
Name: Basic 32-bit Amazon Linux AMI 2011.02.1 Beta
Description: Amazon Linux AMI Base 2011.02.1, EBS boot, 32-bit architecture with Amazon EC2 AMI Tools.   Edit AMI

Number of Instances: 1
Availability Zone: No Preference
Instance Type: Micro (t1.micro)
Instance Class: On Demand   Edit Instance Details

Monitoring: Disabled   **Termination Protection:** Disabled
Tenancy: Default
Kernel ID: Use Default   **Shutdown Behavior:** Stop
RAM Disk ID: Use Default
User Data: Edit Advanced Details

Key Pair Name: Tasklet   Edit Key Pair

Security Group(s): sg-7edbbc17   Edit Firewall

‹ Back   [Launch ▷]

FIGURE E4.12

Parameters that can be enabled for a simple EC2 instance.

Accessing EC2 Using Command-Line Tools Amazon also provides a command-line interface to EC2 that uses the EC2 API to implement specialized operations that cannot be performed with the AWS console. The following briefly describes how to install and set up the command-line utilities. More details are found in *The Amazon Elastic Compute Cloud User Guide*.[9] The details of the command-line tools are found in *The Amazon Elastic Compute Cloud Command Line Reference*.[10]

Download tools: The EC2 command-line utilities can be downloaded from *Amazon EC2 API Tools*[11] as a Zip file. They are written in Java and hence will run on Linux, Unix, and Windows if the appropriate Java Runtime Environment (JRE) is available. To use them, simply unpack the file, then set appropriate environment variables, depending on the operating system being used. These environment variables can also be set as parameters to the command.

NOTE

Installing EC2 command-line tools:
- Download tools.
- Set environment variables (e.g., location of JRE).
- Set security environment (e.g., get certificate).
- Set region.

Set environment variables: The first command sets the environment variable that specifies the directory in which the Java runtime resides. PATHNAME should be the full pathname of the directory where the java.exe file can be found. The second command specifies the directory where the EC2 tools reside; TOOLS_PATHNAME should be set to the full pathname of the directory named ec2-api-tools-A.B-nnn into which the tools were unzipped. (A, B, and nnn are some digits that differ based on the version used.) The third command sets the executable path to include the directory where the EC2 command utilities are present.

```
For Linux:
$export JAVA_HOME = PATHNAME
$export EC2_TOOLS = TOOLS_PATHNAME
$export PATH=$PATH:$EC2_HOME/bin
For Windows:
C:\>SET JAVA_HOME = PATHNAME
C:\>SET EC2_TOOLS = TOOLS_PATHNAME
C:\>SET PATH = %PATH%,%EC2_HOME%\bin
```

Set up security environment: The next step is to set up the environment so that the EC2 command = line utilities can authenticate to AWS during each interaction. To do this, it is necessary to download an X.509 certificate and a private key that authenticates HTTP requests to Amazon. The

---

[9] *Amazon Elastic Compute Cloud User Guide,* http://docs.amazonwebservices.com/AWSEC2/latest/UserGuide/ [accessed 10.11].

[10] *Amazon Elastic Compute Cloud Command Line Reference,* http://docs.amazonwebservices.com/AWSEC2/ latest/CommandLineReference/ [accessed 01.11].

[11] *Amazon EC2 API Tools,* http://aws.amazon.com/developertools/351?_encoding=UTF8&jiveRedirect=1 [accessed 10.11]

X.509 certificate can be generated by clicking on the **Account** link shown in Figure E4.9, clicking on the **Security Credentials** link that is displayed, and following the given instructions to create a new certificate. The certificate files should be downloaded to an `.ec2` directory in the home directory on Linux/Unix and `C:\ec2` on Windows, without changing their names. The following commands are to be executed to set up the environment; both Linux and Windows commands are given. Here, `f1.pem` is the certificate file downloaded from EC2.

```
$export EC2-CERT=~/.ec2/f1.pem
or
C:\> set EC2-CERT=~/.ec2/f1.pem
```

Set region: It is necessary to next set the *region* that the EC2 command tools interact with—that is, the location in which the EC2 virtual machines would be created. In brief, each region represents an AWS datacenter, and AWS pricing varies by region. The command `ec2-describe-regions` can be issued at this point to test the installation of the EC2 command tools and list the available regions.

The default region used is the US-East region **us-east-1**, with service endpoint URL http://ec2.us-east-1.amazonaws.com, but it can be set to any specific endpoint using the following command, where `ENDPOINT_URL` is formed from the region name as illustrated for the **us-east-1**.

```
$export EC2-URL=https://<ENDPOINT_URL>
Or
C:\> set EC2-URL=https://<ENDPOINT_URL>
```

A later section explains how developers can use the EC2 and S3 APIs to set up a Web application to implement a simple publishing portal such as the Pustak Portal. Before that, we need to understand more about what a computation resource is and the parameters that we can configure for each such resource, described in the next section.

EC2 Computational Resources This section gives a brief overview of the computational resources available on EC2, followed by storage and network resources.[12]

Computing resources: The computing resources available on EC2, referred to as *EC2 instances*, consist of combinations of computing power, together with other resources such as memory. Amazon measures the computing power of an EC2 instance in terms of EC2 Compute Units.[13] An *EC2 Compute Unit* (CU) is a standard measure of computing power in the same way that bytes are a standard measure of storage. One EC2 CU provides the same amount of computing power as a 1.0–1.2 GHz Opteron or Xeon processor in 2007. Thus, if a developer requests a computing resource of 1 EC2 CU, and the resource is allocated on a 2.4 GHz processor, they may get 50% of the CPU. This measurement allows developers to request standard amounts of CPU power regardless of the physical hardware.

The EC2 instances that Amazon recommends for most applications belong to the *Standard Instance* family.[12] The characteristics of this family are shown in Table E4.1, "EC2 Standard Instance Types." A developer can request a computing resource of one of the instance types shown in the table (e.g., a small computing instance, which would have the characteristics shown). Figure E4.10 shows how we can do this using the AWS console.

---

[12] *EC2 Introduction, http://aws.amazon.com/ec2/ [accessed 10.11].*
[13] *EC2 FAQs, http://aws.amazon.com/ec2/faqs/ [accessed 10.11].*

Table E4.1 EC2 Standard Instance Types

Instance Type	Compute Capacity	Memory	Local Storage	Platform
Small	1 virtual core of 1 CU	1.7GB	160GB	32-bit
Large	2 virtual cores, 2 CU each	7.5GB	850GB	64-bit
Extra Large	4 virtual cores, 2 CU each	15GB	1690GB	64-bit

Other instance families available in Amazon at the time of this writing include the High-Memory Instance family, suitable for databases and other memory-hungry applications; the High-CPU Instance family for compute-intensive applications; the Cluster-Compute Instance family for High-Performance Compute (HiPC) applications, and the Cluster GPU Instance family, which includes graphic processing units (GPUs) for HiPC applications that need GPUs.[12]

Software: Amazon makes available certain standard combinations of operating system and application software in the form of *Amazon Machine Images* (AMIs). The required AMI has to be specified when requesting the EC2 instance, as seen earlier. The AMI running on an EC2 instance is also called the *root AMI*.

Operating systems available in AMIs include various flavors of Linux, such as Red Hat Enterprise Linux and SuSE, the Windows server, and Solaris. Available software includes databases such as IBM DB2, Oracle, and Microsoft SQL Server. A wide variety of other application software and middleware, such as Hadoop, Apache, and Ruby on Rails, are also available.[12]

There are two ways of using additional software not available in standard AMIs. It is possible to request a standard AMI and then install the additional necessary software. This AMI can then be saved as one of the available AMIs in Amazon. The other method is to import a VMware image as an AMI using the `ec2-import-instance` and `ec2-import-disk-image` commands. For more details of how to do this, the reader is referred to.[13]

Regions and Availability Zones: EC2 offers regions, which are the same as the S3 regions. Within a region, there are multiple availability zones, where each availability zone corresponds to a virtual datacenter that is isolated (for failure purposes) from other availability zones. Thus, an enterprise that wants to have its EC2 computing instances in Europe could select the "Europe" region when creating EC2 instances. By creating two instances in different availability zones, the enterprise could have a highly available configuration that is tolerant to failures in any one availability zone.

Load Balancing and Scaling: EC2 provides the *Elastic Load Balancer*, which is a service that balances the load across multiple servers. The default load-balancing policy is to treat all requests as being independent. However, it is also possible to have timer-based and application-controlled sessions, whereby successive requests from the same client are routed to the same server based on time or application direction.[14] The load balancer also scales the number of servers up or down, depending on the load. This can also be used as a failover policy, since failure of a server is detected by the Elastic Load Balancer. Subsequently, if the load on the remaining server is too high, the Elastic Load Balancer could start a new server instance.

Once the compute resources are identified, we need to set any necessary storage resources.

---

[14] *Elastic Load Balancing, http://aws.amazon.com/elasticloadbalancing/ [accessed 10.11].*

> **NOTE**
>
> **EC2 Storage Resources**
> - Amazon S3: Highly available object store
> - Elastic Block Service: Permanent block storage
> - Instance Storage: Transient block storage

EC2 Storage Resources As stated earlier, computing resources can be used along with associated storage and network resources in order to be useful. Use of the S3 files is similar to accessing an HTTP server (a Web file system). However, often an application performs multiple disk inputs/outputs (IOs), and for performance and other reasons we need to have a control on the storage configuration as well. This section describes how we can configure resources that appear to be physical disks to the EC2 server, called *block storage resources*. There are two types of block storage resource: Elastic Block Service and instance storage, described next.

Elastic Block Service (EBS): In the same way that S3 provides file storage services, EBS provides a block storage service for EC2. It is possible to request an EBS disk volume of a particular size and attach this volume to one or multiple EC2 instances using the instance ID returned during the time the volume is created. Unlike the local storage assigned during the creation of an EC2 instance, the EBS volume has an existence independent of any EC2 instance, which is critical to have persistence of data, as detailed later.

Instance Storage: Every EC2 instance has local storage that can be configured as a part of the compute resource (Figure E4.10); this is referred to as *instance storage*. Table E4.2 shows the default partitioning of instance storage associated with each EC2 instance for standard instance types. This instance storage is ephemeral (unlike EBS storage)—that is, it exists only as long as the EC2 instance exists and cannot be attached to any other EC2 instance. Furthermore, if the EC2 instance is terminated, the instance storage ceases to exist. To overcome this limitation of local storage, developers can use either EBS or S3 for persistent storage and sharing.

Table E4.2 Partitioning of Local Storage in Standard EC2 Instance Types

	Small	Large	Extra Large
Linux	/dev/sda1: root file system	/dev/sda1: root file system	/dev/sda1: root file system
	/dev/sda2: /mnt	/dev/sdb: /mnt/	/dev/sdb: /mnt
	/dev/sda3: /swap	dev/sdc	/dev/sdc
		/dev/sdd	/dev/sdd
		/dev/sde	/dev/sde
Windows	/dev/sda1: C:	/dev/sda1: C:	/dev/sda1: C:
	xvdb	xvdb	xvdb
		xvdc	xvdc
		xvdd	xvdd
		xvde	xvde

Table E4.3 Comparison of Instance Storage and EBS Storage

	Instance Storage	EBS Storage
Creation	Created by default when an EC2 instance is created	Created independently of EC2 instances.
Sharing	Can be attached only to EC2 instance with which it is created.	Can be shared between EC2 instances.
Attachment	Attached by default to S3-backed instances; can be attached to EBS-backed instances	Not attached by default to any instance.
Persistence	Not persistent; vanishes if EC2 instance is terminated	Persistent even if EC2 instance is terminated.
S3 snapshot	Can be snapshotted to S3	Can be snapshotted to S3

The instance AMI, configuration files, and any other persistent files can be stored in S3, and during operation a snapshot of the data can be periodically taken and sent to S3. If data needs to be shared, this can be accomplished via files stored in S3. An EBS storage can also be attached to an instance as desired.

Table E4.3 summarizes some of the main differences and similarities between the two types of storage.

S3-backed instances vs. EBS-backed instances: EC2 compute and storage resources behave slightly differently depending on whether the root AMI for the EC2 instance is stored in Amazon S3 or in Amazon Elastic Block Service (EBS). These instances are referred to as *S3-backed instances* and *EBS-backed instances*, respectively. In an S3-backed instance, the root AMI is stored in S3, which is file storage. Therefore, it must be copied to the root device in the EC2 instance before the EC2 instance can be booted. However, since instance storage is not persistent, any modifications made to the AMI of an S3-backed instance (such as patching the OS or installing additional software) will not be persistent beyond the lifetime of the instance. Furthermore, while instance storage is attached by default to an S3-backed instance (as shown in Table E4.2), instance storage is not attached by default to EBS-backed instances.

EC2 Networking Resources In addition to compute and storage resources, network resources are also needed by applications. For networking between EC2 instances, EC2 offers both a public address as well as a private address [9]. It also offers DNS services for managing DNS names associated with these IP addressees. Access to these IP addresses is controlled by policies. The Virtual Private Cloud can be used to provide secure communication between an intranet and the EC2 network. We can also create a complete logical subnetwork and expose it to a public one (a DMZ) with its own firewall rules. Another interesting feature of EC2 is the Elastic IP addresses, which are independent of any instance; this feature can be used to support failover of servers. These advanced features and how they can be used to set up a network are described in this section, after we outline the key terminologies.

NOTE

EC2 Networking
- Private and public IP addresses per instance
- Elastic IP addresses not associated with any instance
- Route 53 DNS that allows simple URLs (e.g., www.mywebsite.com)
- Security groups for networking security policies

Instance addresses: Each EC2 instance has two IP addresses associated with it: the *public IP address* and the *private IP address*. The private IP address and DNS name can be resolved only within the EC2 cloud. For communication between EC2 instances, the internal IP addresses are most efficient, since the messages then pass entirely within the Amazon network. The public IP address and DNS name can be used for communication outside the Amazon cloud.

Elastic IP addresses: These IP addresses are independent of any instance but are associated with a particular Amazon EC2 account and can be dynamically assigned to any instance (in which case, the public IP address is deassigned). Therefore, they are useful for implementing failover. Upon failure of one EC2 instance, the Elastic IP address can be dynamically assigned to another EC2 instance. Unlike instance IP addresses, Elastic IP addresses are not automatically allocated; they have to be generated when needed.

Route 53: Enterprises may desire to publish a uniform resource locator (URL) of the form www. myenterprise.com for EC2 instances. This is not possible by default, since the EC2 instances are inside the `amazon.com` domain. Route 53 is a DNS server that can be used to associate an Elastic IP address or public IP address with a name of the form www.myenterprise.com.

Security Groups: For networking security, it is common to define network security policies that restrict the ports through which any machine can be accessed or the IP addresses that can access a server. The same can be achieved for EC2 instances using security groups, briefly mentioned earlier. Each security group is a collection of network security policies. Different security groups should be created for different server types; for example, the Web server security group could specify that port 80 may be opened for incoming connections. The default security group, in creating an EC2 instance, allows the instance to connect to any outside IP address but disallows incoming connections.

Virtual Private Cloud: Enterprises that desire more control over their networking configuration can use a *virtual private cloud* (VPC). Examples of the advanced networking features offered by VPCs include:
1. The ability to allocate both public and private IP addresses to instances from any address range
2. The ability to divide the addresses into subnets and control the routing between subnets
3. The ability to connect the EC2 network with an Intranet using a VPN tunnel.

Details of VPCs are beyond the scope of this book and can be found in *Amazon Virtual Private Cloud*.[15]

A Simple EC2 Example: Setting Up a Web Server

Now let's look at all the terminologies and concepts described in the previous two sections in the context of a simple example of creating a Web server. The Web server will be created as an EBS-backed instance, to avoid the necessity of having to periodically back up the storage to S3.

The process is broken down into four steps:
1. Select the AMI for the instance.
2. Create the EC2 instance and install the Web server.
3. Create an EBS volume for data, such as HTML files and so on.
4. Set up networking and access rules.

It is assumed that the data needed for the Web server (HTML files, scripts, executables, and so on) are available and have been uploaded to EC2. Furthermore, to illustrate how to install

---

[15] *Amazon Virtual Private Cloud*, http://aws.amazon.com/vpc/ [accessed 10.11].

custom software on a standard AMI, it is assumed that the necessary Web server also has to be uploaded to EC2 and then installed. (In reality, a Web server instance may be available as an image as well.)

Selecting the AMI Instructions to create a new EC2 instance using the AWS console were described earlier. The user may recall that one step during this process is selecting an AMI (discussed around Figure E4.10). More details of this phase to perform advanced functionality are described next.

Using the drop-down menus to select **Amazon Images** and **Amazon Linux** brings up a list of Linux images supplied by Amazon, as shown in Figure E4.13. Here the Root Device column indicates whether the root device for the image is EBS or not. Some of the important parameters of the AMI are in the Description tag in the lower half of the figure. It can be seen that the image is a 64-bit Amazon Linux image with the root device /dev/sda1 in EBS. The value true in the Block Devices field is the DeleteUponTerminate flag and indicates that the device is not persistent— that is, it will vanish if the EC2 instance terminates. Clicking the Launch button brings up the launch wizard, which goes through a number of steps (such as selecting the size of the machine and possibly creating a new key pair) before launching the EC2 instance. However, at the time of this writing, there is no way to create an EC2 instance with a persistent root device through the AWS Console. Therefore, the next section describes how to launch the EC2 instance using the command line.

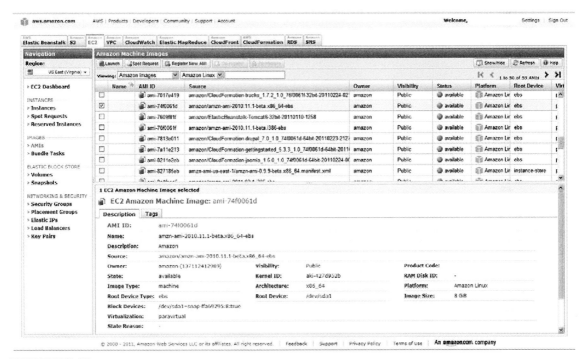

FIGURE E4.13

Selecting an AMI.

Creating the Example EC2 Instance Two other important steps done during the creation of an instance are (1) generate a key pair that provides access to the EC2 servers that are created and (2) create a security group that will be associated with the instance and specify the networking access rules. In our example, since the created instance will not have the required software (Web server) installed on it by default, the created security group will initially be an empty security group that disallows any incoming network access. Subsequently, the security group will be modified to allow HTTP access.

The key pair is generated from the EC2 console (see Figure E4.13) by clicking on the **Key Pair** link, following the instructions, and downloading the resulting files (called `f2.pem` in this example). The following script shows how to set an environment variable named `EC2-PRIVATE-KEY` so as to make the downloaded key the default key-pair for EC2 instances.

```
For Linux:
$export EC2-PRIVATE-KEY=~/.ec2/f2.pem
$ec2addgrp "Web Server" –d "Security Group for Web Servers"
$ec2run ami-74f0061d –b dev/sda1=::false –k f2.pem –g "Web Server"
For Windows:
C:\> set EC2-PRIVATE-KEY=C:\.ec2\f2.pem
C:\> ec2addgrp "Web Server" –d "Security Group for Web Servers"
C:\> ec2run ami-74f0061d –b "xvda=::false" –k f2.pem –g "Web Server"
```

In this example, the `ec2addgrp` command (short for `ec2-create-group`) creates a security group called Web Server and disallows all external access. As stated earlier, this rule will later be modified to allow HTTP access. Next, the `ec2run` command (short form for the `ec2-run-instances` command) is used to start the instance with a persistent EBS root volume. The first parameter is the AMI ID of the AMI selected in Figure E4.13. The value `false` in the –b flag (which controls the behavior of the root volume) indicates that the `DeleteUponTerminate` flag for this volume is to be set to `false`. This implies that the volume will not be deleted even if the EC2 instance terminates. The –k and –g parameters specify the key pair that can be used to communicate with the instance and the security group for the instances, respectively. The number of instances to be launched defaults to 1. A range can be explicitly specified using the `-instance-count` parameter. More details of all the command-line options for EC2 are available at *The Amazon Elastic Compute Cloud Command Line Reference*[10].

The DNS name for the newly created instance is available from AWS console. Alternatively, the `ec2-describe-instances` command (`ec2din` is the short form) can be also used to get the public DNS name of the instance. Subsequently, ssh, PuTTY, or Remote Desktop Connection can be used to log in to the instance and download the software to be installed (via yum, for example). After installing the additional software, the image can be saved on EBS as an AMI using the `ec2-create-instance` command. The parameter `instanceId` is the instance ID of the EC2 instance, and the command returns the AMI ID of the newly created EBS AMI. These steps are shown in the following script:

```
For Linux:
$ec2din
$ssh –i f2.pem instance-id
$ec2-create-instance –n "Web Server AMI" instanceId
For Windows:
C:\>ec2-describe-instances
C:\putty
C:\>ec2-create-instance –n "Web Server AMI" instanceId
```

Attaching an EBS Volume Since the HTML pages to be served from the Web portal need to be persistent, it is required to create an EBS volume for holding the HTML pages that are to be served by the Web server. EBS volumes can be created from the EC2 console (see Figure E4.13) by clicking on the **Volumes** link. This brings up a list of all EBS volumes currently owned by the user. Clicking the **Create Volume** button brings up the screen shown in Figure E4.14, where the size of the needed volume can be specified before being created.

The new volume that has been created is shown on the Volumes screen with a status of Available (see masked content on Figure E4.15). Clicking on the **Attach Volume** button brings up the

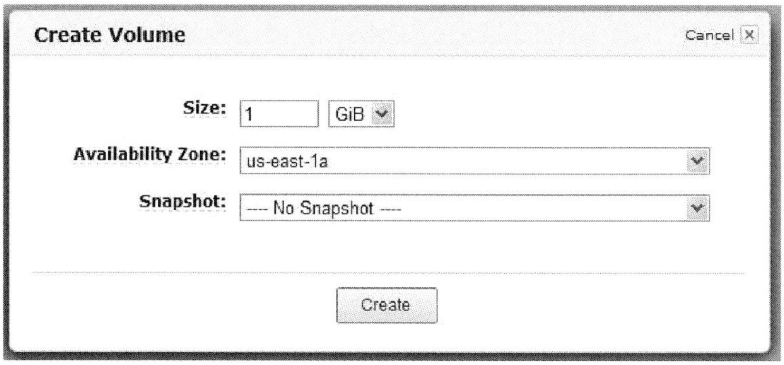

FIGURE E4.14
Creating an EBS volume.

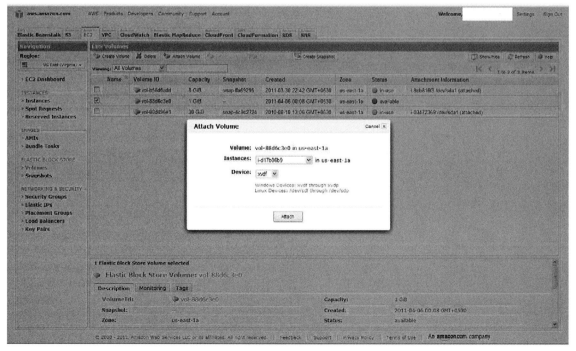

FIGURE E4.15
Attaching an EBS volume to an EC2 instance.

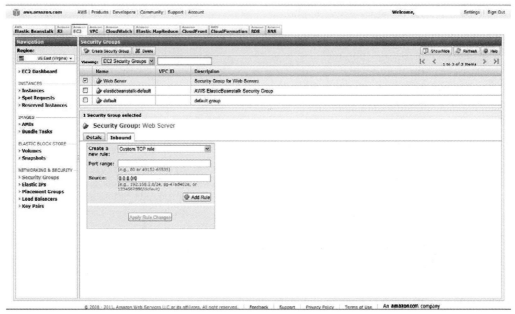

FIGURE E4.16
Modifying a security group.

Attach Volume screen (Figure E4.15), which has drop-down menus for the EC2 instance to be used as well as the device name (`xvdf` to `xvdp` for Windows, `/dev/sdf` to `/dev/sdp` for Linux). After making the appropriate selections, clicking the **Attach** button will virtually attach the volume to the selected instance. At this stage, an EC2 instance has been created, the Web server has been installed, and a separate persistent store on EBS has been attached.

Allowing External Access to the Web Server Since the Web server is now ready for operation, external access to it can now be enabled. Clicking on the **Security Groups** link at the left of the EC2 console brings up a list of all available security groups. Figure E4.16 shows the available security groups, which consist of the newly created group Web Server and two default groups. By clicking on the **Inbound** tab, it is possible to input rules that specify the type of traffic allowed. Figure E4.16 shows how to add a new rule that allows traffic on port 80 from all IP addresses (specified by the 0 IP address). A specific IP address can also be typed in to allow a specific IP address to be allowed. Clicking the **Add Rule** button adds this particular rule. After all rules are added, clicking the **Apply Rule Changes** button activates the newly added rules. By permitting external access to the Web server, it is effectively in a DMZ, a region in an intranet where external access is allowed.[16,17] Similarly, by disallowing external access from outside to other servers, they are effectively kept out of the DMZ.

This completes the deployment of a simple Web server on EC2 and EBS.

---

[16] *AWS Security Best Practices, http://awsmedia.s3.amazonaws.com/pdf/AWS_Security_Whitepaper.pdf; 2011 [accessed 10.11].*
[17] *Fernandes R. Creating DMZ configurations on Amazon EC2, http://tripoverit.blogspot.com/2011/03/creating-dmz-configurations-on-amazon.html [accessed 10.11].*

ADDITIONAL SERVICE MODELS

As mentioned before, the cloud is a collection of services. New services are constantly being created to meet user needs. These services lead to new service models in addition to the three traditional models. Although there are numerous other service models, we cover only two here: Database as a Service (DbaaS) and Desktop as a Service (DaaS).

Database as a Service

DbaaS provides a database platform organizations can use to store their data. Many PaaS providers also provide database services, but in many instances organizations do not need a development platform; they simply need a place to store data. In these cases, a DbaaS option is a good choice. Although storage prices are coming down, the cost is still pretty high. A DbaaS implementation would include the database platform and the storage you need at a cost lower than what you could implement internally.

Desktop as a Service

DaaS is one of the newer service models being provided. In general, DaaS provides users with a virtual desktop that can be used to perform desktop computing. Companies are still trying to figure out the best way to provide this type of service and what features and functionality they need to provide along with it. One of the big questions is whether pooled desktops will provide an adequate user experience or whether dedicated desktops are needed to provide an adequate user experience.

Storage as a Service

Data is the lifeblood of an enterprise. Enterprises have varied requirements for data, including structured data in relational databases that power an e-commerce business or documents that capture unstructured data about business processes, plans, and visions. Enterprises may also need to store objects, such as an online photo album or a collaborative document-editing platform, on behalf of their customers. Furthermore, some of the data may be confidential and must be protected; other data should be easily shareable. In all cases, business-critical data should be secure and available on demand in the face of hardware and software failures, network partitions, and inevitable user errors.

NOTE

Amazon Storage Services
- Simple Storage Service (S3): An object store
- SimpleDB: A key-value store
- Relational Database Service (RDS): MySQL instance

Amazon Simple Storage Service (S3)

Amazon Web Services (**AWS**), from Amazon.com, has a suite of cloud service products that have become very popular and are almost looked up to as a *de facto* standard for delivering IaaS. Figure E4.17 shows a screen shot of AWS, depicting its various IaaS products in multiple tabs (S3, EC2, CloudWatch).

Amazon S3 is a highly reliable, highly available, scalable, and fast storage in the cloud for storing and retrieving large amounts of data through simple Web services. This section gives some preliminary details of the platform and then takes a simple example using S3, followed by a detailed description of S3 features.[18] More advanced uses of S3 are described in a later section on Amazon EC2, with an example of how S3 APIs can be used by developers together with other Amazon compute services (such as EC2) to form a complete IaaS solution.

First, a look at how we can use S3 as a simple cloud storage tool to upload files.

Accessing S3 There are three ways of using S3. Most common operations can be performed via the AWS console, the GUI interface to AWS (shown in Figure E4.17) that can be accessed via http://aws.amazon.com/console. For use of S3 within applications, Amazon provides a REST-ful API with familiar HTTP operations such as GET, PUT, DELETE, and HEAD. Also, there are libraries and SDKs for various languages that abstract these operations.

FIGURE E4.17
AWS Console.

---

[18] *Amazon Simple Storage Service (Amazon S3), http://aws.amazon.com/s3 [accessed 16.10.11].*

Additionally, since S3 is a storage service, several *S3 browsers* exist that allow users to explore their S3 account as though it were a directory (or a folder). There are also file system implementations that let users treat their S3 accounts as just another directory on their local disk. Several command-line utilities[19,20] that can be used in batch scripts also exist and are described toward the end of this section.

Getting Started with S3 Let's start with a simple personal-use case. Consider a user who has a directory full of personal photos that she wants to store in the cloud for backup. Here's how this could be approached:

1. Sign up for S3 at http://aws.amazon.com/s3/. While signing up, obtain the **AWS Access Key** and the **AWS Secret Key**. These are similar to the user ID and password combination that is used to authenticate all transactions with Amazon Web Services (not just S3).
2. Sign in to the **AWS Management Console** for S3 (see Figure E4.17) at https://console.aws.amazon.com/s3/home.
3. Create a *bucket* (see Figure E4.18) giving a name and geographical location where it can be stored. In S3 all files (called *objects*) are stored in a bucket, which represents a collection of related objects. Buckets and objects are described later in the section "Organizing Data in S3: Buckets, Objects and Keys."
4. Click the **Upload** button (see Figure E4.19) and follow the instructions to upload files.
5. The photos or other files are now safely backed up to S3 and available for sharing with a URL if the right permissions are provided.

From a developer perspective, this can also be accomplished programmatically in case there is a need to include this functionality in a program.

Organizing Data in S3: Buckets, Objects, and Keys Files are called *objects* in S3. Objects are referred to with keys—basically, an optional directory path name followed by the name of the object. Objects in S3 are replicated across multiple geographic locations to make them resilient to several types of failures (however, consistency across replicas is not guaranteed). If object versioning is enabled, recovery from inadvertent deletions and modifications is possible. S3 objects can be up to 5 terabytes in size and there are no limits on the number of objects that can be stored. All objects in S3 must be stored in a bucket. Buckets provide a way to keep related objects in one place and separate them from others. There can be up to 100 buckets per account and an unlimited number of objects in a bucket.

Each object has a key, which can be used as the path to the resource in an HTTP URL. For example, if the bucket is named `johndoe` and the key to an object is `resume.doc`, then its HTTP URL is http://s3.amazonaws.com/johndoe/resume.doc or, alternatively, http://johndoe.s3.amazonaws.com/resume.doc. By convention, slash-separated keys are used to establish a directory-like naming scheme for convenient browsing in S3 explorers such as the AWS Console, S3Fox, and so

[19] s3cmd: command line S3 client, http://s3tools.org/s3cmd [accessed 10.11].
[20] Standalone Windows .EXE command line utility for Amazon S3 & EC2, http://s3.codeplex.com/ [accessed 10.11].

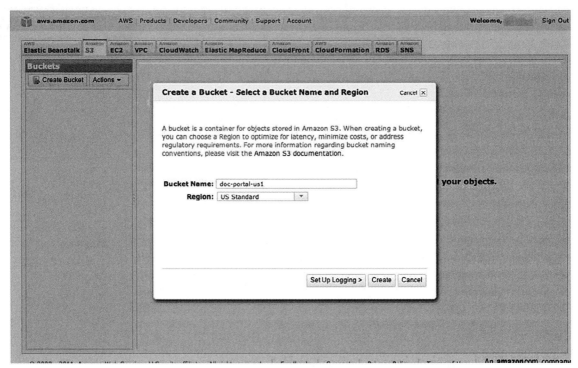

FIGURE E4.18
Creating a bucket.

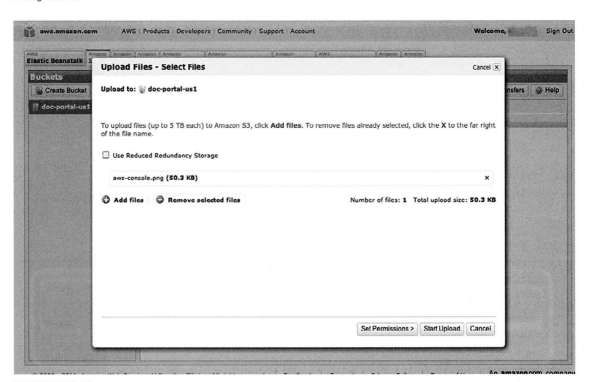

FIGURE E4.19
Uploading objects.

on. For example, we can have URLs such as http://johndoe.s3.amazon.aws.com/project1/file1.c, http://johndoe.s3.amazon.aws.com/project1/file2.c, and http://johndoe.s3.amazon.aws.com/project2/file1.c. However, these are files with keys (names) `project1/file1.c`, and so on, and S3 is not really a hierarchical file system. Note that the bucket namespace is shared; it is not possible to create a bucket with a name that has already been used by another S3 user.

Note that entering the preceding URLs into a browser will not work as expected; not only are these values fictional, but even if real values were substituted for the bucket and key, the result would be an "HTTP 403 Forbidden" error. This is because the URL lacks authentication parameters; S3 objects are private by default, and requests should carry authentication parameters that prove the requester has rights to access the object, unless the object has Public permissions. Typically the client library, SDK, or application will use the AWS Access Key and AWS Secret Key (described later) to compute a signature that identifies the requester and append this signature to the S3 request. For example, the S3 *Getting Started Guide* is stored in the `awsdocs` bucket at the `S3/latest/s3-gsg.pdf` key with anonymous read permissions; hence it is available to everyone at http://s3.amazonaws.com/awsdocs/S3/latest/s3-gsg.pdf.

S3 Administration In any enterprise, data is always coupled to policies that determine the location of the data and its availability as well as who can and cannot access it. For security and compliance with local regulations, it is necessary to be able to audit and log actions and be able to undo inadvertent user actions. S3 provides facilities for all of these, described as follows:

Security: Users can ensure the security of their S3 data by two methods. First, S3 offers *access control* to objects. Users can set permissions that allow others to access their objects. This is accomplished via the AWS Management Console. A right-click on an object brings up the object actions menu (see Figure E4.20). Granting anonymous read access to objects makes them readable by anyone; this is useful, for example, for static content on a web site. This is accomplished by selecting the *Make Public* option on the object menu. It is also possible to narrow read or write access to specific AWS accounts. This is accomplished by selecting the *Properties* option that brings up another menu (not shown) that allows users to enter the email IDs of users to be allowed access. It is also possible to allow others to put objects in a bucket in a similar way. A common use for this action is to provide clients with a way to submit documents for modification, which are then written to a different bucket (or different keys in the same bucket) where the client has permissions to pick up the modified document

The other method that helps secure S3 data is to collect audit logs. S3 allows users to turn on *logging* for a bucket, in which case it stores complete access logs for the bucket in a different bucket (or, if desired, in the same bucket). This allows users to see which AWS account accessed the objects, the time of access, the IP address from which the accesses took place, and the operations that were performed. Logging can be enabled from the AWS Management Console (Figure E4.21). Logging can also be enabled at the time of bucket creation.

Data protection: S3 offers two features to prevent data loss.[18] By default, S3 replicates data across multiple storage devices and is designed to survive two replica failures. It is also possible to request **Reduced Redundancy Storage(RRS)** for non-critical data. RRS data is replicated twice and is designed to survive one replica failure. It is important to note that Amazon does not guarantee consistency among the replicas; that is, if there are three replicas of the data, an application reading a replica that has a delayed update could read an older version of the data.

Versioning: If versioning is enabled on a bucket, S3 automatically stores the full history of all objects in the bucket from that time onward. The object can be restored to a prior version, and even deletes can be undone. This guarantees that data is never inadvertently lost.

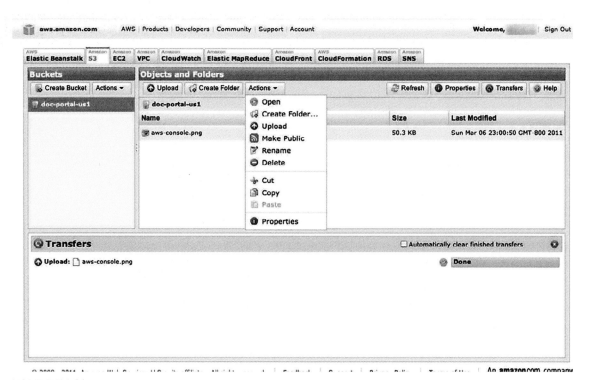

FIGURE E4.20

Amazon S3: Performing actions on objects.

FIGURE E4.21

Amazon S3 bucket logging.

Regions: For performance, legal, and other reasons, it may be desirable to have S3 data running in specific geographic locations. This can be accomplished at the bucket level by selecting the region in which the bucket is stored during its creation. The region corresponds to a large geographic area, such as the United States (California) or Europe. The current list of regions can be found on the S3 Website.[18]

Large Objects and Multipart Uploads The object size limit for S3 is 5 terabytes, which is more than is required to store an uncompressed 1080p HD movie. In the instance that this is not sufficient, the object can be stored in smaller chunks with the splitting and recomposition being managed in the application using the data.

Although Amazon S3 has high aggregate bandwidth available, uploading large objects will still take some time. Additionally, if an upload fails, the entire object needs to be uploaded again. Multipart upload solves both problems elegantly. S3 provides APIs that allow the developer to write a program that splits a large object into several parts and uploads each part independently.[21] These uploads can be parallelized for greater speed to maximize the network utilization. If a part fails to upload, only that part needs to be retried. S3 supported up to 10,000 parts per object as of writing of this book.

Amazon Simple DB Unlike Amazon S3, which provides file-level operations, *SimpleDB* (SDB) provides a simple data store interface in the form of a key-value store. SDB allows storage and retrieval of a set of attributes based on a key. Use of key-value stores is an alternative to relational databases that use SQL-based queries. It is a type of NoSQL data store. The next section provides a short overview of SDB.

Data Organization and Access Data in SDB is organized into domains. Each item in a domain has a unique key that must be provided during creation. Each item can have up to 256 attributes, which are name-value pairs. In terms of the relational model, for each row the primary key translates to the item name and the column names and values for that row translate to the attribute name-value pairs. For example, if it is necessary to store information regarding an employee, it is possible to store the attributes of the employee (e.g., the employee name) indexed by an appropriate key, such as an employee ID. Unlike a relational database management system (RDBMS), attributes in SDB can have multiple values—for example, if in a retail product database the list of *keywords* for each item in the product catalog can be stored as a single value corresponding to the attribute `keywords`, doing this with an RDBMS would be more complex.

SDB provides a query language that is analogous to SQL, although there are methods to fetch a single item. Queries take advantage of the fact that SDB automatically indexes all attributes.

SDB Availability and Administration SDB has a number of features to increase availability and reliability. Data stored in SDB is automatically replicated across different geographies for high availability. It also automatically adds compute resources in proportion to the request rate and automatically indexes all fields in the dataset for efficient access. SDB is schemaless; that is, fields can be added to the dataset as the need arises.

Amazon Relational Database Service

Amazon Relational Database Service (RDS) provides a traditional database abstraction in the cloud, specifically a MySQL instance in the cloud. An RDS instance can be created using the RDS tab in the AWS Management Console (see Figure E4.22).

---

[21] *API Support for Multipart Upload*, http://docs.amazonwebservices.com/AmazonS3/ latest/dev/index. html?uploadobjusingmpu.html [accessed 01.11].

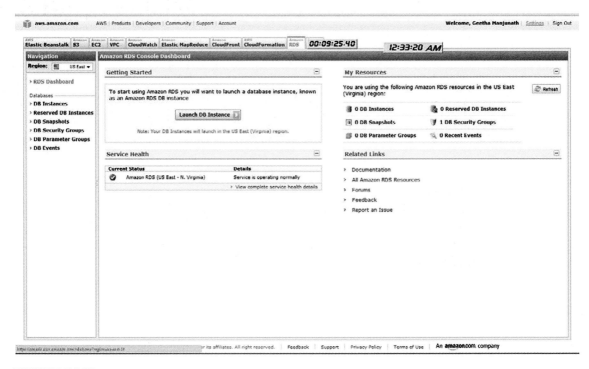

FIGURE E4.22
AWS Console: Relational database service.

AWS performs many of the administrative tasks associated with maintaining a database for the user. The database is backed up at configurable intervals, which can be as frequent as 5 minutes. The backup data is retained for a configurable period of time, which can be up to eight days. Amazon also provides the capability to snapshot the database as needed. All these administrative tasks can be performed through the AWS console (as in Figure E4.22). Alternatively, it is possible to develop a custom tool that will perform the tasks through the Amazon RDS APIs.

SUMMARY

NIST has outlined three main cloud service models: SaaS, PaaS, and IaaS. The SaaS model has been around the longest. It dates back to the old ASP days. Each service model has its own benefits and drawbacks. One thing you must be careful with when you choose a service model is what you as the customer will be responsible for. Whether you are using a cloud provider or not, you must always ensure that you have accounted for the maintenance and monitoring of your systems and applications. The only difference with a cloud model is that there are certain aspects that the provider will be responsible for. Whatever the case, you need to make sure these things are accounted for.

Making the Decision

INTRODUCTION

Choosing the right cloud scenario and the right provider the first time can be critical to your organization's success. Depending on the provider, once you have made your choice, you might be stuck, because it could be extremely difficult for you to move your data to another provider.

If the IT department chooses the wrong provider, they risk losing credibility with the business. One of draws of public cloud environments is that the business can consume the services directly. They do not have to rely on their internal IT department. If an organization's IT department loses credibility, there is a good chance that the business will begin bypassing them altogether.

TO GO TO THE CLOUD OR NOT?

The first step in evaluating a move to the cloud is to determine what problem you are trying to solve. You could be solving some sort of technical or functional issue, or you could be trying to solve the problem of how you can offer your customers a new service or capability.

You need to determine whether the service you need is something you can do yourself. But just because you *can* do it doesn't mean you *should*. Some people take the stance that if it's not an offering that's core to your business or what you do well, you should consider moving it to a service provider. This is especially true for services that cost a lot to support and maintain.

You need to determine what your expectations would be for a provider. You need to be realistic and figure out whether there is a provider that could possibly meet your needs. Sometimes your expectations may be so unrealistic that no provider could possibly meet them.

Another key point you must consider is how often you plan on using the services. If you will use them on a regular basis, it might be more cost effective to implement the services yourself. Remember, on the cloud you will be paying for usage, so using the services on a regular basis could be very costly.

CHOOSING A CLOUD SERVICE MODEL

After you figure out the basics of what you want to do, you need to figure out which service model best fits your needs. This might not be as simple as you think. For example, just because you need application services doesn't mean you choose a SaaS provider. You may choose a PaaS provider and build the application yourself.

So, let's look at some of the things you must consider in choosing your service model.

User Experience

User experience can play a big role in your decision. After all, your end goal is to service clients. If your clients are not satisfied, then your implementation will not be a successful one.

If it's important for you to have control over the user experience, a public SaaS model might not be a good option for you. In a SaaS model, you will have very little control over the UI. You will also have very little opportunity to customize the application for your users.

If you go with a PaaS or an IaaS implementation, you will have complete control over the application. You can make any customization you need to the application. Other factors, such as, network bandwidth, may play a part in determining the user experience. Without appropriate bandwidth, the system may seem slow or unresponsive.

Security

When talking about public clouds, the various cloud service models offer different levels of security. This mainly centers around who has control over what. Keep in mind that there are two different scenarios to consider. The first is keeping your data safe from external threats. The second is keeping your data safe from potential threats at the provider.

In a SaaS environment, the provider has complete control over and access to all data, and there is very little you can do to protect it. At the other end of the spectrum is IaaS. In an IaaS environment, the provider has physical access to the data, but there are methods you can put in place to protect that data, such as implementing data encryption.

Compliance

Most organizations have at least some compliance regulations to which they must adhere. Compliance regulations can put a burden on your IT systems and infrastructure. Many people look to the cloud to help lessen that burden. Each cloud service model varies in the degree to which it can help you adhere to your compliance regulations.

In an SaaS model, the provider will assume a large portion of the compliance burden. Depending on the compliance required, the SaaS provider may assume all of the burden. Your organization may still be liable from a legal standpoint, but the provider will assume the burden of making sure its systems comply.

In a PaaS model, the burden is shared. The provider will ensure that the compliance regulations are met by the platform and the hardware. The customer must ensure that the compliance regulations are met by the application that is built. This can be a somewhat tricky area. A lot of due diligence must be performed to determine whether the entire implementation is compliant.

In an IaaS model, most of the burden falls on the customer. But this also means that in an IaaS model, the customer will have the greatest confidence that the appropriate compliancy measures have been taken.

CHOOSING A CLOUD DEPLOYMENT MODEL

After you have chosen the cloud service model that best fits your need, you need to determine your cloud deployment model. You can choose from among public, private, community, and hybrid. Most people believe that the hybrid cloud model is the model that will be used in most organizations. However, you still must consider which model is best for your organization.

User Experience

The cloud offers different user experiences depending on which deployment model you choose.

If you choose to go with a private cloud, you will complete control over the user experience. You will be able to control the application, the network, and, in most cases, the client systems. This allows you to tune everything for best performance and usability.

If you go with a public cloud, in some cases you might have no control over the user experience. In a community cloud environment, your control over the user experience depends on the agreement you have in place with the other members of the community.

Security

Security is always a complicated topic. It's even more complicated when you're dealing with the cloud. It mainly comes down to trust. Whom do you trust with your security? Many organizations would rather trust a third party than trust themselves. There is absolutely nothing wrong with that. Security is such an important concern that you need to go with what you trust.

Responsibilities

Responsibilities vary greatly depending on which cloud model you intend to go with. This can be another key factor in your decision. In fact, one of the big drivers of public clouds is organizations' desire to reduce their internal responsibilities.

The following tables outline who is responsible for what in each environment configuration. Table 5.1 outlines SaaS provider responsibilities.

Table 5.1 SaaS Responsibilities by Cloud Deployment Model

	Public	Private	Community	Hybrid
Application Updates	Provider	Consumer	Consumer	Varies
OS Updates	Provider	Consumer	Consumer	Varies
Antivirus	Provider	Consumer	Consumer	Varies
Storage	Provider	Consumer	Consumer	Varies
Networking	Provider	Consumer	Consumer	Varies
Physical Server Hardware	Provider	Consumer	Consumer	Varies
Client Application	Consumer	Consumer	Consumer	Varies
Client System	Consumer	Consumer	Consumer	Varies

Table 5.2 outlines PaaS provider responsibilities.

Table 5.2 PaaS Responsibilities by Cloud Deployment Model

	Public	Private	Community	Hybrid
Application Updates	Consumer	Consumer	Consumer	Varies
OS Updates	Provider	Consumer	Consumer	Varies
Antivirus	Varies	Consumer	Consumer	Varies
Storage	Provider	Consumer	Consumer	Varies
Networking	Provider	Consumer	Consumer	Varies
Physical Server Hardware	Provider	Consumer	Consumer	Varies
Client Application	Consumer	Consumer	Consumer	Varies
Client System	Consumer	Consumer	Consumer	Varies

Table 5.3 outlines IaaS provider responsibilities.

Table 5.3 IaaS Responsibilities by Cloud Deployment Model

	Public	Private	Community	Hybrid
Application Updates	Consumer	Consumer	Consumer	Varies
OS Updates	Varies	Consumer	Consumer	Varies
Antivirus	Consumer	Consumer	Consumer	Varies
Storage	Provider	Consumer	Consumer	Varies
Networking	Provider	Consumer	Consumer	Varies
Physical Server Hardware	Provider	Consumer	Consumer	Varies
Client Application	Consumer	Consumer	Consumer	Varies
Client System	Consumer	Consumer	Consumer	Varies

CHOOSING A PUBLIC CLOUD SERVICE PROVIDER

If you decide to go with a public cloud provider, you have to determine which one you will use. There are different things you must consider in evaluating the various types of providers. We cover some of the more important criteria here.

Tips for Choosing a SaaS Provider

In most cases, SaaS providers offer different applications. This means that you will have to evaluate both the application and the service provider. The following questions are some you should ask as you are considering a SaaS provider:

- How will you be charged?
- Can bulk data imports/exports be done?

- How are data migrations handled?
- How hard would it be to move to a new provider if necessary?
- Find out what ability you will have to customize the application.
- Find out what downtime you can expect. When is scheduled maintenance?
- What performance and availability SLAs exist? What are the penalties for violating these SLAs?
- What insight will you gain into what's going on with the application and the data? Can you gather your own metrics? Do your own monitoring?

Tips for Choosing a PaaS Provider

Although service providers may offer different platforms, with PaaS you might find that you can get the same platform from different providers. The following questions are some you should ask when you're considering a PaaS provider:

- How will you be charged?
- What operating system, development, and database platform does the provider offer?
- Is the platform compatible with the applications and/or services you want to deliver?
- Find out what downtime you can expect. When is scheduled maintenance?
- What performance and availability SLAs exist? What are the penalties for violating these SLAs?
- What insight will you gain into what's going on with the application and the data? Can you gather your own metrics? Do your own monitoring?

Tips for Choosing an IaaS Provider

Most IaaS providers offer the same infrastructure platforms. So the key is to find a provider that offers a service that most appeals to you. The following questions are some you should ask when you're considering an IaaS provider:

- How will you be charged?
- Does the provider provide all the infrastructure components you need? Will you need to supplement them in some way?
- What insight will you gain into what's going on with the application and the data? Can you gather your own metrics? Do your own monitoring?
- Find out what downtime you can expect. When is scheduled maintenance?
- What performance and availability SLAs exist? What are the penalties for violating these SLAs?
- Is any software included as part of the plan?
- How are data migrations handled?

CHAPTER 6

Evaluating Cloud Security: An Information Security Framework

Cloud security represents yet another opportunity to apply sound security principles and engineering to a specific domain and to solve for a given set of problems. This chapter builds on our previous discussions and presents the foundation for a framework for evaluating cloud security. It should benefit activities that precede the evaluation, certification, or accreditation of a cloud.

We start by reviewing existing work in this area, and then we put forward a set of checklists of evaluation criteria that span the range of activities that together support information security for cloud computing. The goal of this chapter is to provide the reader with an organized set of tools that can be used to evaluate the security of a private, community, public, or hybrid cloud. Evaluating the security of a hybrid cloud may best be done by managing the evaluation of the two or more cloud instances using one set of checklists per instance. For example, if the hybrid consists of a private cloud and a public cloud, simply evaluate the private components using one set of checklists and evaluate the public components into their separate realms. In this manner, you can more readily compare public cloud alternatives.

EVALUATING CLOUD SECURITY

Most users of a cloud, whether a private or a public cloud, have certain expectations for the security of their data. Similarly, the owner and operator of a cloud share responsibility for ensuring that security measures are in place and that standards and procedures are followed. We can capture our expectations and responsibilities for security by stating them formally in documented requirements. By example, the NIST 800-53 security controls detail specific requirements for federal government systems. Systems that are fielded by government agencies must generally comply with these and related NIST requirements. The Cloud Security Alliance *Controls Matrix* takes a similar approach in detailing security requirements for cloud implementations, and there is a growing trend by commercial users to adopt such generally accepted requirements. A good starting point when you need to measure the presence and effectiveness of the security of a cloud includes having a list of required or recommended security controls.

To begin, there are two aspects to security controls in cloud implementations. The first has to do with the presence of the control. The second aspect is the effectiveness or robustness of the control. In other words, it is not enough that a security control is present; that control also needs to be effective. Going further, one can describe this as the degree of trust (or assurance) that can be expected from these controls. For instance, a cloud may implement encrypted communications between the cloud and an external user— but if we are evaluating the effectiveness of encrypted communications, we also need to verify that the control is properly designed, implemented, and verified.

Measuring the presence and/or effectiveness of security controls (against security requirements) is largely what security evaluations are intended to do. Security evaluations have broad value as guidance for planning or developing security and for verifying that required controls are properly implemented. But evaluations also have utility for procurement of cloud services; for instance, a cloud provider may choose to publish the high-level results of a third-party security evaluation. In addition, if we are to compare the security of two or more clouds, that will entail having a common set of criteria for evaluation.

On the basis of the sensitivity of data or the expected risk of a system, we should undergo an initial requirements phase where appropriate security controls are identified. If we subsequently perform a thorough assessment of the decision process that led to identifying those controls and couple that assessment with a security evaluation of the effectiveness of those controls that were implemented, we should gain a fairly good understanding of whether an overall cloud service has a sound security posture versus the risk to which it is subject.

Figure 6.1 depicts the relationship between requirements, security evaluation of a cloud, the cloud implementation, vulnerability remediation, and continuing configuration management controls.

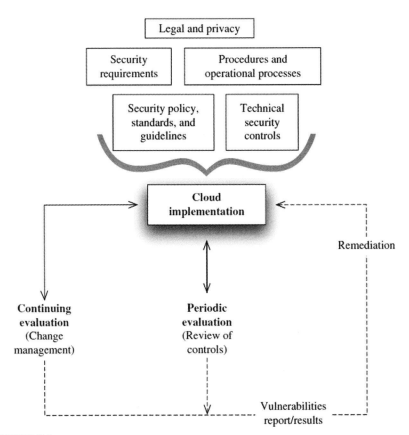

FIGURE 6.1
From Requirements and Evaluation to Ongoing Security Remediation

Existing Work on Cloud Security Guidance or Frameworks

In the few years since cloud computing arrived as a new model for IT, several efforts have already taken place to offer guidance for cloud security. These efforts include:

- *Cloud Security Alliance (CSA)*. The CSA has been very active in various efforts, including:
  - *Cloud Controls Matrix (CCM)*. This effort is "designed to provide fundamental security principles to guide cloud vendors and to assist prospective cloud customers in assessing the overall security risk of a cloud provider. The Cloud Controls Matrix provides a controls framework that gives detailed understanding of security concepts and principles that are aligned to the Cloud Security Alliance guidance in 13 domains."[1]

- *Consensus Assessments Initiative Questionnaire.* This effort is "focused on providing industry-accepted ways to document what security controls exist in IaaS, PaaS, and SaaS offerings, providing security control transparency."[2]
- *Security Guidance for Critical Areas of Focus in Cloud Computing.* V2.1, published in December 2009, presented security guidance for a number of areas in cloud computing; these areas include architecture, governance, traditional security, and virtualization.
- *Domain 12: Guidance for Identity & Access Management.* V2.1, published in April 2010, discusses the major identity management functions as they relate to cloud computing. This work forms a cornerstone of the CSA's *Trusted Cloud Initiative.*

- *CloudAudit.* Seeks to give cloud adopters and cloud operators the tools to measure and compare the security of cloud services. It does this by defining "a common interface and namespace that allows cloud computing providers to automate the Audit, Assertion, Assessment, and Assurance (A6) of their infrastructure (IaaS), platform (PaaS), and application (SaaS) environments."[3]
- *European Network and Information Security Agency (ENISA).* Leading the security guidance efforts in Europe, ENISA has produced several guiding publications for securely adopting cloud computing. These include:
  - *Cloud Computing: Information Assurance Framework.* Published in November 2009. Presents a set of assurance criteria that address the risk of adopting cloud computing.
  - *Cloud Computing: Benefits, Risks and Recommendations for Information Security.* Published in November 2009.
  - *The Federal CIO Council's Proposed Security Assessment and Authorization for U.S. Government Cloud Computing.*[4] The core importance of this document is that it adopts the NIST 800-53R3 security controls for cloud computing in low- and moderate-risk systems.
- *The Trusted Computing Group (TCG).* In September 2010, the TCG formed the *Trusted Multi-Tenant Infrastructure Work Group,* which is intended to develop a security framework for cloud computing. The Trusted Multi-Tenant Infrastructure Work Group will use existing standards to define end-to-end security for cloud computing in a framework that can serve as a baseline for compliance and auditing.

All these efforts are relatively new and have yet to gain broad acceptance. More so, they are either initial activities that are intended to serve as a starting point for more formal work or the product of community efforts toward a common framework for cloud security. In other words, there is a great deal of uncertainty in this area. That presents a difficulty for cloud adopters who need to evaluate the security of their private or community clouds and for users who need a means to evaluate the security of a cloud service.

Today, users do not yet have a common and standard means to evaluate cloud security. In fact, much of the pre–cloud computing world has not adopted security evaluation frameworks outside those realms where regulation requires a security benchmark or where evaluation is mandated. But cloud security is a fast-moving area, and all the efforts we've cited took place between 2009 and the end of 2010. The adoption of these efforts is accelerating in several ways, especially in the government space with FedRAMP. By its very nature, adoption of public clouds is a change agent in security. There is a fast-shaping trend here, and we can expect to see real progress in the near term. This is an example of how cloud computing is stimulating better security in business areas where otherwise there was great concern over security but little improvement until the rise of public clouds.

TOOLS

Many tools are used for security testing. These include the following categories:

- Port scanning for open and responding services
- Simple Network Management Protocol (SNMP) scanning
- Device enumeration or cataloging
- Host vulnerability scanning
- Network device analysis
- Password compliance testing and cracking

There are several basic tools that have stood the test of time. These include Network Mapper (NMAP) for port scanning and Nessus for host vulnerability scanning. In addition, there has been a more recent crop of powerful tools that allow for extensive defense testing to identify quality, resiliency, and related security vulnerabilities. These tools offer test suites for a broad range of cloud network security needs.

CHECKLISTS FOR EVALUATING CLOUD SECURITY

The intent of developing a cloud security evaluation checklist is to have a uniform means to verify the security of a cloud and to obtain assurance from a CSP about their security. However, as stated in this chapter's introduction, such checklists can also be used by prospective customers or users to compare the cloud security options offered by different providers.

The remainder of this section presents checklists that form the heart of a framework for evaluating cloud security. The questions in these checklists are derived from several sources, including the CSA Cloud Controls Matrix,[5] the ENISA Cloud Computing Information Assurance Framework,[6] and NIST's 800-53R3.[7]

One application for the checklist is that a cloud owner can use it to guide a security evaluation of its cloud. If cloud providers use such a checklist as a framework to report on the security of their clouds, then prospective tenants and users can compare the relative security of multiple clouds. The checklist can also be used by a public cloud customer to ask a series of questions that are relevant to the customer's business needs. Not all these questions will be relevant for all uses or business relationships.

Each of the following sections is organized around a set of closely related controls or requirements. Figure 6.2 presents an overview of the evaluation checklist sections and lists the groups of controls or requirements for each section.

FOUNDATIONAL SECURITY

A *security policy* defines the organization's requirements or rules for security. A security policy delineates the constraints and requirements that individuals and groups must operate under, and it serves as a statement of management's intent for security. Actions that are taken in regard to security should be clearly traceable to the security policy. Several classes of policy may exist, including an overall security policy as well as additional policies that address more limited

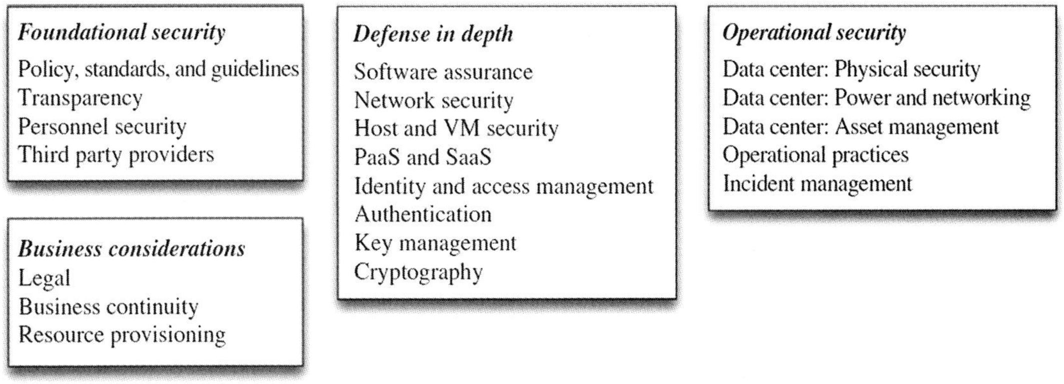

Foundational security	Defense in depth	Operational security
Policy, standards, and guidelines Transparency Personnel security Third party providers	Software assurance Network security Host and VM security PaaS and SaaS Identity and access management Authentication Key management Cryptography	Data center: Physical security Data center: Power and networking Data center: Asset management Operational practices Incident management

Business considerations
Legal Business continuity Resource provisioning

FIGURE 6.2
Overview of Evaluation Checklist

areas (such as an *acceptable-use policy*). The security policy is focused on achieving desired results, not on specific implementations.

Augmenting such policies are other statements of requirements for specific areas. These are usually defined as *standards* and cover such specific areas as technical controls or specific hardening requirements. Standards state mandatory actions that support policy. *Guidelines* are a third class of documentation that is less formal and more oriented toward procedural best practices. These are recommendations or descriptions of practices that support the objectives of a security policy by describing a framework to implement procedures. In other words: A policy states *why*, a standard states *what*, and a guideline states *how*. Checklist 6.1 covers foundational security elements related to policy, standards, and guidelines. Checklist 6.2 covers evaluation criteria that are focused on CSP transparency.

CHECKLIST 6.1: POLICY, STANDARDS, AND GUIDELINES[8–10]

- Has a security policy been clearly documented, approved, and represented to all concerned parties as representing management's intent?
- Has the security policy had legal, privacy, and other governance review?
- Has the security policy been augmented by security standards and/or guidelines?
- Has the policy been augmented by a privacy policy?
- Are the security and privacy policies, as well as standards and guidelines, consistent with industry standards (such as 27001, CoBIT, and so on)?
- Are third-party providers held to the same policies and standards?

CHECKLIST 6.2: TRANSPARENCY[11–13]

- Does the CSP provide customers with a copy of the governing policies, standards, and guidelines?
- Are customers notified of changes to governing policies, standards, and guidelines?
- Does the CSP provide customers with visibility into third-party compliance audits?
- Does the CSP provide customers with visibility into penetration tests?
- Does the CSP provide customers with visibility into internal and external audits?
- Does the CSP provide customers with visibility into CSP asset management and repurposing of equipment?

Personnel security for a cloud is a foundation on which operational security resides. The intent of personnel security is to avoid several classes of security risk and to create an environment that reinforces the objectives that are stated in security policy. Checklist 6.3 lists evaluation criteria related to personnel security.

CHECKLIST 6.3: PERSONNEL SECURITY[14–16]

- Are there policies and procedures for:
  - Hiring employees who will have access to or control over cloud components?
  - Pre-employment checks for personnel with privileged access?
- Are personnel security policies consistent across locations?
- Do they apply to online cloud systems and data as well as to offline systems that either stored data or to offline systems that will be provisioned for online use?
- Is there a security education program, and if so, how extensive is it?
- Is personnel security frequently reviewed to determine whether employees with access should continue to have access?
- Are personnel required to have and maintain security certifications?
- Does physical access to the CSP's facility require background checks?

The use of subcontractors or third-party providers can create undue risk for customers unless such providers follow and operate in accordance with CSP policies. Checklist 6.4 details criteria for third-party providers.

CHECKLIST 6.4: THIRD-PARTY PROVIDERS[17–19]

- Are any services or functions provided by a third party?
- If any part of a cloud is subcontracted or otherwise outsourced, does the providing party comply with the same policy and standards that the CSP enforces?
- If used, are third-party providers audited for compliance with the CSP's policies and standards?
- Does the CSP security policy (or equivalent) and governance extend to all third-party providers?

BUSINESS CONSIDERATIONS

Various business considerations bring with them the need for security considerations. Business considerations include legal issues, business continuity, and resource provisioning. Evaluation criteria for these considerations are listed in Checklists 6.5 (legal issues), 6.6 (business continuity), and 6.7 (resource provisioning).

CHECKLIST 6.5: LEGAL[20–22]

- Where—in which jurisdiction—will data be stored?
- Where—in which jurisdiction—is the CSP incorporated?
- Does the CSP use third-party providers who are not located in the same jurisdiction?
- Does the CSP subcontract any services or personnel?
- Does the CSP use a customer's data in any manner that is not part of the service?
- Does the CSP have a documented procedure for responding to legal requests (such as a subpoena) for customer data?
- In the event of a subpoena, how does the CSP produce data for a single customer only without providing nonsubpoena data?
- Is the CSP insured against losses, including remuneration for customer losses due to CSP outages or data exposure?

Business continuity can be critical for customers who use cloud-based services in a mission-critical manner. Criteria associated with business continuity are listed in Checklist 6.6.

CHECKLIST 6.6: BUSINESS CONTINUITY[23–25]

- Does the CSP have a formal process or contingency plan that documents and guides business continuity?
- What are the service recovery point objective (RPO) and recovery time objective (RTO)?
- Is information security integral to recovery and restoration?
- How does the CSP communicate a disruption of services to customers?
- Is there a secondary site for disaster recovery?

Business continuity is a complex topic that warrants far greater coverage than is possible in a cloud security book. The interested reader is encouraged to research several related topic areas, including business continuity planning along with contingency and disaster recovery planning. There are many sources in these areas, including:

- ANSI/ASIS SPC.1-2009 Organizational Resilience: Security, Preparedness, and Continuity Management Systems—Requirements with Guidance for Use American National Standard
- The National Institute of Science and Technology (NIST) Special Publication 800-34, *Contingency Planning Guide for Information Technology Systems*

- Good Practice Guidelines, which can be downloaded from www. thebcicertificate.org/bci_gpg.html
- The Business Continuity Institute, located online at www.thebci.org

Epic Fail

As reported by the German online newspaper *Zeit Online*[26] on February 18, 2011, an error in a cloud provider's payment system paralyzed a German company's access to its public cloud SaaS email and online documents. Although the actual facts in this case were not fully clear at the time this chapter was written, it should serve as a warning: Any cloud provider's accounting or customer management systems could be in error, and in an extreme case this might result in a *business* denial-of-service situation.

Such an accounting error is certainly not unique in the world of billing and debt collection, but in a communications system—such as the Internet—or in a cloud services situation, the error can conceivably occur, and the consequences will be felt very quickly, without the victim having any prior billing warning. The cloud services model brings a second complicating factor: Many cloud services largely rely on self-service interfaces, with little recourse from traditional human customer service representatives.

In the radio.de case, it appears that the CSP abruptly cut off access to radio.de's office software and relevant documents. Radio.de apparently could not reach the CSP's regional office in Dublin, and emails to the CSP did not solve the problem for a few days. The facts in this specific case are not at all clear, so the CSP will go unidentified here. However, if you outsource your critical business functions, make certain that any similar situation can be more quickly resolved with the CSP. That will entail doing your homework before you form a business relationship with a CSP, and it will entail maintaining contact with the provider so that you are always aware of any changes in contact methods or details. Finally, consider this: If your disaster recovery plan is stored on the CSP's systems, you really don't have a CSP disaster recovery plan at all.

Resource provisioning has to do with assuring that the cloud service will be sufficiently resourced as customer demand increases. To do this, a CSP would need to take certain measures to successfully deliver on its SLAs. For instance, the CSP might have procedures in place to add servers or storage as demand increases. Checklist 6.7 lists evaluation criteria for resource provisioning.

CHECKLIST 6.7: RESOURCE PROVISIONING[27–29]
- What controls and procedures are in place to manage resource exhaustion, including processing oversubscription, memory or storage exhaustion, and network congestion?
- Does the CSP limit subscriptions to the service in order to protect SLAs?
- Does the CSP provide customers with utilization and capacity planning information?

DEFENSE IN DEPTH

The integrity and security of an operational cloud depends on the integrity of components that comprise it. Software is a primary vector for vulnerabilities and exploits. To begin, Checklist 6.8 lists evaluation criteria for software assurance.

CHECKLIST 6.8: SOFTWARE ASSURANCE[30–32]

- What controls are in place to maintain integrity of operating systems, applications, firmware updates, configuration files, and other software?
- What industry standards, guidelines, or best practices are followed?
- What controls or guidelines are used to obtain or download software and configuration files?
- What guidelines or procedures are used to maintain software integrity?
- Is penetration or vulnerability testing used on each release?
- How are identified vulnerabilities remediated?

One very powerful technique for improving software security is to empower developers during the development process itself by giving them access to security testing tools. Such tools range from static code analysis through Web security testing. A best practice is to have the development environment closely mirror the eventual testing, staging, and production environments. With development, this is not always easy, but the fewer deltas between environments, the better the transition and the fewer security surprises your developers will encounter. (When test, staging, and production environments vary widely, errors and costs will rise dramatically as well.)

TIP

One software testing technique is known as *fuzzing*. This technique involves injecting invalid and unexpected data to the input of a program or system. Using this technique, even random data can result in program crashing or entering a state whereby a security control can be made to fail. Two areas are especially fruitful for this testing: One is file formats, and the other is network protocols. Fuzz data can be sent as events, command-line input, or mutated packets. One of the strengths of using fuzzing is that it can illuminate severe and exploitable bugs.

The most significant aspect of a cloud's security may well be the network implementation. Architectural and isolation choices that are made here will have far-reaching benefits or consequences. Network choices start with the physical network and equipment functionality and extend to network virtualization and monitoring. The degree of isolation between different classes of traffic (customer access, customer-to-customer, operations and management, external access, and so on) will drive other security requirements at the systems and VM levels. Checklist 6.9 lists criteria for network security.

CHECKLIST 6.9: NETWORK SECURITY[33–35]

- What controls are in place to manage externally sourced and internally sourced attacks, including distributed denial of service (DDoS)?
- For customers, how is isolation managed between virtual machines (VMs) by the hypervisor?
- For customers, how is isolation managed between VMs by network hardware and routing?
- What standards or best practices are used to implement virtual network infrastructure?
- How are Media Access Control (MAC) spoofing, Address Resolution Protocol (ARP) poisoning, and so on protected against?
- How is isolation managed between customer-accessed/routable systems and cloud management systems and infrastructure?
- Is cloud customer processing dependent on off-cloud tenant components such as Lightweight Directory Access Protocol (LDAP)?
- Does the CSP perform periodic penetration testing against the cloud?
- If so, is penetration testing done both external to the cloud and from inside the cloud and the cloud infrastructure?
- Does the CSP perform vulnerability testing of the cloud infrastructure, cloud management, and customer accessible components?
- How are identified vulnerabilities tracked and addressed?
- Is vulnerability information made available to customers?
- Does the CSP allow customers to perform vulnerability testing against the customer's own VMs or other containers?

The kinds and degree of security controls that are required to protect hosts and VMs are to a large extent driven by the network architecture. On one hand there are trade-offs between extreme network isolation and control and on the other hand with the desire for maximum flexibility in operation. The greater the flexibility, the more compensating controls are needed at the host and VM levels. Checklist 6.10 lists evaluation criteria for host and VM security.

CHECKLIST 6.10: HOST AND VM SECURITY[36–38]

- Are customer VMs encrypted and/or otherwise protected when stored?
- Are VM images patched before they are provisioned?
- How and how frequently are VM images patched after being provisioned?
- To which standards or guidelines are VM images hardened before being provisioned?
- What are the procedures for protecting hardened and patched VM images?
- Can a customer provide its own VM image?
- Does the CSP include any authentication credentials, and if so, what are they used for?
- Do hardened and patched VM images include operating firewall instances by default? (And if so, what are the allowed services/ports?)
- Do hardened and patched VM images include operating intrusion detection systems (IDSs) or intrusion prevention systems (IPSs)?
- If so, does the CSP have access to these in operation (and if so, how)?
- Do hardened and patched VM images include any form of network, performance, or security instrumentation that the CSP or tenant has access to?
- How is isolation ensured between server-colocated VMs for different customers?

- How is communication implemented between VMs for the same customer?
- How is security ensured for user data in storage systems?
- How is security ensured for user data in motion between storage systems and customer VMs?
- How is security ensured for user data and user interaction between a VM and a noncloud user system?
- Does the CSP provide information to customers to guide customer security so that it is appropriate for the virtualized environment?

CSPs are generally responsible for the platform software stack, including security. Although a CSP may be reluctant to provide details about the security of a PaaS stack, a CSP should be transparent about its security practices and the scope of security controls. Checklist 6.11 lists evaluation criteria for PaaS and SaaS security.

CHECKLIST 6.11: PAAS AND SAAS SECURITY[39–41]
- How does the CSP isolate multitenant applications?
- How does the CSP isolate a user's or tenant's data?
- How does the CSP identify new security vulnerabilities in applications and within the cloud infrastructure?
- Does the CSP provide security as a service feature for PaaS (such as authentication, single sign-on, authorization, and transport security)?
- What administrative controls does the CSP provide to a tenant/user, and do these controls support defining/enforcing access controls by other users?
- Does the CSP provide separate test and production environments for customers?

Identity and access management are critical elements of security for a cloud. Checklist 6.12 lists evaluation criteria for identity and access management, along with authentication.

CHECKLIST 6.12: IDENTITY AND ACCESS MANAGEMENT[42–44]
- Do any CSP controlled accounts have cloud-wide privileges (and if so, which operations)?
- How does the CSP manage accounts with administrator or higher privilege?
- Does the CSP use two-man access controls, and if so, for which operations?
- Does the CSP enforce privilege separation (for instance, Role-Based Access Control, or RBAC), and if so, what roles are used to limit which privileges (security, OS admin, identity, and so on)?
- Does the CSP implement break-glass access, and if so, under what circumstances and what is the process for post-cleanup?
- Does the CSP grant tenants or users administrator privileges, and if so, what are the limits to these privileges?
- Does the CSP verify user identity at registration, and if so, are there different levels of checks, depending on resources to which access is granted?
- How are credentials and accounts deprovisioned?

- Is deprovisioning of credentials and accounts done in a cloud-wide atomic-operation manner?
- How is remote access managed and implemented?

For CSP-supplied customer-use identity and access management systems:

- Does this support federated identity management?
- Is the CSP's system interoperable with third-party identity provider systems?
- Can a customer incorporate single sign-on?
- Does this system support separation of roles and least privilege principal (LPP)?

How does a CSP verify its identity to a customer under the following scenarios?

- When the CSP communicates out-of-band to a customer or user
- When a customer interacts with the CSP via an API
- When a customer uses a cloud management interface

Authentication:

- How is authentication implemented for high-assurance CSP operations?
- Is multifactor authentication used?
- Is access to high-assurance operations limited to only operations cloud-networks and only from whitelisted IP addresses?
- Does intrusion detection/anomaly detection detect multiple failed logins or similarly suspicious authentication or credential compromise activities?
- What procedures are invoked if customer credentials or accounts are compromised?

Key management and cryptography must be handled in precise and correct ways; otherwise, cryptographic security is quickly undermined. Checklist 6.13 lists security criteria for these areas.

CHECKLIST 6.13: KEY MANAGEMENT AND CRYPTOGRAPHY[45–47]

Key management for keys that the CSP controls:

- How does the CSP protect keys, and what security controls are in place to affect that?
- Are hardware security modules used to protect such keys?
- Who has access to such keys?
- How are those keys protected for sign and encrypt operations?
- What procedures are in place to manage and recover from the compromise of keys?
- Is key revocation performed in a cloud-wide atomic operation?

Cryptography:

- For what operations (and where) is encryption used?
- Are all encryption mechanisms based on third-party tested and evaluated products?
- Does security policy clearly define what must be encrypted?

To this point in the checklists, we have covered evaluation criteria for foundational security, business considerations, and defense in depth. The final group of checklists addresses operational security issues.

OPERATIONAL SECURITY

Many concerns around public clouds have to do with the fact that physical security of IT is in a third party's control. With a public cloud, a physical breach will affect multiple customers. Checklist 6.14 lists evaluation criteria for datacenter physical security and datacenter power and networking.

CHECKLIST 6.14: DATACENTER PHYSICAL SECURITY, POWER, AND NETWORKING[48–50]

Datacenter physical security:

- What are the requirements for being granted physical access to the CSP's facility?
- Do non-employees require escort in the facility?
- Is entry into the facility constrained by function and entry location? (Examples: shipping and receiving, housekeeping)
- Is the facility divided into zones such that each requires access permissions?
- Is strong authentication (for example, multifactor card and PIN or card and biometric) required for physical access?
- Is all access monitored and documented?
- Are all entry locations alarmed and monitored?
- Is video monitoring complete for all common areas of the facility?
- How long is video retained?
- How often is a risk assessment performed for physical security?
- Does the CSP require that all deliveries or equipment removals be performed by the CSP within the facility (that is, is there a separate shipping facility outside the physical perimeter of the cloud facility itself)?

Datacenter power and networking:

- Is power and networking secured within the facility?
- Are environmental systems (lighting, air conditioning, fire detection) implemented to industry standards?
- Is air conditioning sized to withstand extended periods of extreme conditions?
- Is the facility exposed to moderate or higher risk of environmental or weather damage?
- Does the facility receive power from multiple power sources?
- Does the facility provide backup power generation for a period or time that is adequate to recover from loss of a primary power source?
- Does the facility have adequate uninterruptible power supply (UPS) for short or temporary outages?
- Does the facility have multiple Internet connections and are these from different tier 1 providers?

A CSP must maintain a current and complete list of all information resources that are used to implement and operate the cloud. The state-of-the-practice (ITIL) is to use a configuration management database (CMDB) to maintain such information. The state of the art is to have that process automated by using the CMDB as the centralized repository with which all other cloud management functions interoperate. Checklist 6.15 lists criteria for datacenter asset management.

CHECKLIST 6.15: DATACENTER ASSET MANAGEMENT[51-53]

- Does the CSP maintain a current and complete inventory of all hardware, network, software, and virtual components that comprise the cloud?
- Does the CSP automate such inventory tracking and management?
- Does the CSP maintain a record of all assets that a customer has used or on which a customer has stored data?
- Does the CSP support asset categories of different sensitivity levels, and if so, how are these isolated or separated from each other?
- Does the CSP maintain segregation or physical separation of assets at different sensitivity levels?

Effective security is an ongoing process that entails well-defined procedures and roles for all personnel. To be effective, such procedures must anticipate various kinds of events. Procedures should offer enough guidance to allow personnel to navigate a broad range of failure in systems, processes, and other circumstances. Such events and responses must be captured, with learned lessons integrated into updated procedures. Chapter 7 provides a deeper treatment of this topic, but here we outline the kinds of controls that guide operational practices and security. Checklist 6.16 lists evaluation criteria for operational practices.

CHECKLIST 6.16: OPERATIONAL PRACTICES[54-56]

- Is there a formal change control process, and are the procedures clearly documented?
- Does change control include a means to guide decisions as to what changes require a reassessment of risk?
- Are operating procedures clearly documented and followed?
- Are there separate environments for development, testing, staging, and production?
- What system and network security controls are used to secure end user or tenant applications and information?
- What security controls are used to mitigate malicious code?
- What are the backup procedures (who does this, what gets backed up, how often is it done, what form does it take, and are backups periodically tested)?
- Where are backups stored, and for how long are they kept?
- Will the CSP securely delete all copies of customer data after termination of the customer's contract?
- Under what circumstances are customer resources sanitized using industry best practices (for example, degaussing)?
- Does the CSP have documented security baselines for every component that comprises the cloud infrastructure?

The goal of incident management and response is to minimize or contain the impact of events. Incident management should be well defined in order to support and guide the CSPs and the customer's ability to reduce the consequence of unanticipated events or situations. Checklist 6.17 lists evaluation criteria for the area of incident management.

CHECKLIST 6.17: INCIDENT MANAGEMENT[57-59]

- What information is captured in audit, system, and network logs?
- How long is the information retained, and who has access to it?
- What controls are used to protect these logs from unauthorized access and to preserve the chain of custody of such materials?
- How and how often are logs reviewed?
- How and how often are logs checked for integrity and completeness?
- Are all systems and network components synchronized to a single time source (Network Time Protocol, or NTP)?
- Does the CSP have a formal process to detect, identify, and respond to incidents?
- Are these processes periodically tested to verify that they are effective and appropriate?
- Is log and other security data maintained to comply with legal requirements for chain-of-custody control, and do the data and controls comply with legally admissible forensic data?
- What is the escalation process for incident response?
- Does the CSP use intrusion detection, security monitoring, or Security Event and Incident Management (SEIM) to detect incidents?
- Does a CSP accept customer events and incident information into their security monitoring and incident management process?
- Does the CSP offer transparency into incident events, and if so, what kind of information is shared with customers and users?
- How are security events and security logs protected and maintained?
- How long are security logs retained?
- Who has access to such logs?
- Does the CSP allow customers to implement a host-based IDS in VMs?
- If so, can a customer send such VM IDS data to the CSP for processing and storage?
- How are incidents documented as they take place?
- How are incidents analyzed after the incident has ended?
- Can the CSP provide a forensic image of a customer VM?
- Does the CSP report statistics on incidents to customers?

METRICS FOR THE CHECKLISTS

The checklists alone have utility to judge the security of a cloud, but what prospective public cloud customers and owners of a private cloud want to know are:

- How secure is the implementation?
- Is the CSP meeting best practices for security?
- How well does the CSP meet discrete security controls and requirements?
- How does this service compare with other similar services?

Looking at Checklists 6.1 to 6.17, there is a good deal of variation in how controls can be implemented and how they can be measured. This makes it very difficult to identify metrics for each question. Existing approaches for measuring security meet this challenge by both detailing fine-grained security controls for specific realms (such as NIST 800-53R3) and specifying which of these controls apply to systems operating at different levels of assurance or sensitivity. But even then, the actual evaluation of the security of an implementation is time consuming and expensive and requires expertise.

The resulting certification and accreditation (C&A) of a system is a snapshot in time and must be repeated as the system evolves and undergoes change. Typically, these evaluations are paper exercises that involve a great deal of effort. What is needed is an evolution to this process itself, and cloud computing will demand greater automation, simply due to the nature of the contract between IT and cloud consumers.

What would this look like? To begin with, the information and the evidence *artifacts* that are collected about security, systems, and processes must be organized in a C&A repository that is more like a database than a traditional formal document. The importance of collecting and organizing this information is that it supports statements and claims about how discrete security controls are met.

Having such information in database form makes it useful to multiple entities. In a cloud implementation, multiple parties use the same infrastructure and controls. A security evaluation should enable the reuse of information about such controls as well as information about their effectiveness. Cloud computing really does change the game for security, and it is already becoming clear that the adoption of a cloud will drive the development of not only better security to meet the demands of elasticity and on-demand self-service but also for the measurement and evaluation of security.

SUMMARY

The rise in public computing utilities has brought increased need for better security. By their very nature, competitive public cloud services are faced with the need to provide cost-effective services and features sets that enable ease of adoption. But equally important is the need for a public cloud service to be seen as an appropriate and safe solution to meeting IT requirements. And in that, CSPs have few alternatives other than to undergo evaluation of their product using commonly accepted criteria. Likewise, with private clouds, even if security requirements are included from the earliest design stages and even when sound principles are followed in building and fielding a private cloud, the proverbial proof is still in the *evaluation pudding*.

The security checklists in this chapter are intended to guide readers in developing their own lists for verifying the security of either a CSP or a private cloud. At the time this book was being written, there were several ongoing activities around developing industry or government guidelines around this need. Readers are encouraged to research the state of such work by following the various leading groups that are involved in these activities. It is not at all clear how successful any of these groups will be, and already today there is a good deal of collaboration between groups such as the CSA and CloudAudit/A6. It is certain that this is a rapidly evolving area, and it is very likely that the unique characteristics of the cloud computing model will drive far greater automation in the ongoing verification of such evaluation criteria.

> **NOTE**
>
> Readers who are interested in cloud security evaluation are advised to join the following groups:
> - The Cloud Security Alliance:
>   - www.cloudsecurityalliance.org
>   - www.linkedin.com/groups?mostPopular=&gid=1864210
>   - http://groups.google.com/group/cloudsecurityalliance
> - CloudAudit:
>   - www.cloudaudit.org
>   - http://groups.google.com/group/cloudaudit
> - The Trusted Computing Group:
>   - www.trustedcomputinggroup.org/solutions/cloud_security
>   - www.linkedin.com/groups?mostPopular=&gid=3254114
> - CloudSecurity.org (http://cloudsecurity.org/forum/index.php) is not very active but has potential as an independent forum for collaboration in testing cloud security.

It seems that every few weeks, LinkedIn and Google Groups are adding new cloud groups, and more than a few of these groups are focused on security. With all these cloud security groups, one of the best ways to stay informed is to join the major high-level cloud interest groups and follow general trends in the field. Periodic research via Web searching should identify other specific interest groups as they arise.

Endnotes

1. CSA-GRC-Stack-v1.0-README.pdf; www.cloudsecurityalliance.org.
2. Ibid.
3. Ibid.
4. Proposed Security Assessment & Authorization for U.S. Government Cloud Computing, Draft version 0.96, CIO Council, US Federal Government; 2010.
5. Controls Matrix (CM), Cloud Security Alliance V1.0; 2010.

6. Catteddu D., Hogben G. Cloud Computing Information Assurance Framework, European Network and Information Security Agency (ENISA). www.enisa.europa.eu; 2009 [accessed 24.03.11].

7. NIST Special Publication 800-53 Revision 3, Recommended Security Controls for Federal Information Systems and Organizations; 2009.

8. Controls Matrix (CM), Cloud Security Alliance V1.0; 2010.

9. Catteddu D., Hogben G. Cloud Computing Information Assurance Framework, European Network and Information Security Agency (ENISA). www.enisa.europa.eu; 2009.

10. NIST Special Publication 800-53 Revision 3, Recommended Security Controls for Federal Information Systems and Organizations; 2009.

11. Controls Matrix (CM), Cloud Security Alliance V1.0; 2010.

12. Catteddu D., Hogben G. Cloud Computing Information Assurance Framework, European Network and Information Security Agency (ENISA). www.enisa.europa.eu; 2009.

13. NIST Special Publication 800-53 Revision 3, Recommended Security Controls for Federal Information Systems and Organizations; 2009.

14. Controls Matrix (CM), Cloud Security Alliance V1.0; 2010.

15. Catteddu D., Hogben G. Cloud Computing Information Assurance Framework, European Network and Information Security Agency (ENISA). www.enisa.europa.eu; 2009.

16. NIST Special Publication 800-53 Revision 3, Recommended Security Controls for Federal Information Systems and Organizations; 2009.

17. Controls Matrix (CM), Cloud Security Alliance V1.0; 2010.

18. Catteddu D, Hogben G. Cloud Computing Information Assurance Framework, European Network and Information Security Agency (ENISA). www.enisa.europa.eu; 2009.

19. NIST Special Publication 800-53 Revision 3, Recommended Security Controls for Federal Information Systems and Organizations; 2009.

20. Controls Matrix (CM), Cloud Security Alliance V1.0; 2010.

21. Catteddu D, Hogben G. Cloud Computing Information Assurance Framework, European Network and Information Security Agency (ENISA). www.enisa.europa.eu; 2009.

22. NIST Special Publication 800-53 Revision 3, Recommended Security Controls for Federal Information Systems and Organizations; 2009.

23. Controls Matrix (CM), Cloud Security Alliance V1.0; 2010.

24. Catteddu D, Hogben G. Cloud Computing Information Assurance Framework, European Network and Information Security Agency (ENISA). www.enisa.europa.eu; 2009.

25. NIST Special Publication 800-53 Revision 3, Recommended Security Controls for Federal Information Systems and Organizations; 2009.

26. Asendorpf D. "Ab in die Wolken", Zeit Online, 2011; www.zeit.de/2011/08/ Cloud-Computing; 2011 [accessed 24.03.11].

27. Controls Matrix (CM), Cloud Security Alliance V1.0; 2010.

28. Catteddu D., Hogben G. Cloud Computing Information Assurance Framework, European Network and Information Security Agency (ENISA). www.enisa.europa.eu; 2009.

29. NIST Special Publication 800-53 Revision 3, Recommended Security Controls for Federal Information Systems and Organizations; 2009.

30. Controls Matrix (CM), Cloud Security Alliance V1.0; 2010.

31. Catteddu D., Hogben G. Cloud Computing Information Assurance Framework, European Network and Information Security Agency (ENISA). www.enisa.europa.eu; 2009.

32. NIST Special Publication 800-53 Revision 3, Recommended Security Controls for Federal Information Systems and Organizations; 2009.

33. Controls Matrix (CM), Cloud Security Alliance V1.0; 2010.

34. Catteddu D., Hogben G. Cloud Computing Information Assurance Framework, European Network and Information Security Agency (ENISA). www.enisa.europa.eu; 2009.

35. NIST Special Publication 800-53 Revision 3, Recommended Security Controls for Federal Information Systems and Organizations; 2009.

36. Controls Matrix (CM), Cloud Security Alliance V1.0; 2010.

37. Catteddu D., Hogben G. Cloud Computing Information Assurance Framework, European Network and Information Security Agency (ENISA). www.enisa.europa.eu; 2009.

38. NIST Special Publication 800-53 Revision 3, Recommended Security Controls for Federal Information Systems and Organizations; 2009.

39. Controls Matrix (CM), Cloud Security Alliance V1.0; 2010.

40. Catteddu D., Hogben G. Cloud Computing Information Assurance Framework, European Network and Information Security Agency (ENISA). www.enisa.europa.eu; 2009.

41. NIST Special Publication 800-53 Revision 3, Recommended Security Controls for Federal Information Systems and Organizations; 2009.

42. Controls Matrix (CM), Cloud Security Alliance V1.0; 2010.

43. Catteddu D., Hogben G. Cloud Computing Information Assurance Framework, European Network and Information Security Agency (ENISA). www.enisa.europa.eu; 2009.

44. NIST Special Publication 800-53 Revision 3, Recommended Security Controls for Federal Information Systems and Organizations; 2009.

45. Controls Matrix (CM), Cloud Security Alliance V1.0; 2010.

46. Catteddu D, Hogben G. Cloud Computing Information Assurance Framework, European Network and Information Security Agency (ENISA). www.enisa.europa.eu; 2009.

47. NIST Special Publication 800-53 Revision 3, Recommended Security Controls for Federal Information Systems and Organizations; 2009.

48. Controls Matrix (CM), Cloud Security Alliance V1.0; 2010.

49. Catteddu D., Hogben G. Cloud Computing Information Assurance Framework, European Network and Information Security Agency (ENISA). www.enisa.europa.eu; 2009.

50. NIST Special Publication 800-53 Revision 3, Recommended Security Controls for Federal Information Systems and Organizations; 2009.

51. Controls Matrix (CM), Cloud Security Alliance V1.0; 2010.

52. Catteddu D., Hogben G. Cloud Computing Information Assurance Framework, European Network and Information Security Agency (ENISA). www.enisa.europa.eu; 2009.

53. NIST Special Publication 800-53 Revision 3, Recommended Security Controls for Federal Information Systems and Organizations; 2009.

54. Controls Matrix (CM), Cloud Security Alliance V1.0; 2010.

55. Catteddu D., Hogben G. Cloud Computing Information Assurance Framework, European Network and Information Security Agency (ENISA). www.enisa.europa.eu; 2009.

56. NIST Special Publication 800-53 Revision 3, Recommended Security Controls for Federal Information Systems and Organizations; 2009.

57. Controls Matrix (CM), Cloud Security Alliance V1.0; 2010.

58. Catteddu D., Hogben G. Cloud Computing Information Assurance Framework, European Network and Information Security Agency (ENISA). www.enisa.europa.eu; 2009.

59. NIST Special Publication 800-53 Revision 3, Recommended Security Controls for Federal Information Systems and Organizations; 2009.

CHAPTER 7

Operating a Cloud

- From Architecture to Efficient and Secure Operations
- Security Operations Activities

Throughout this book and in several ways, we have stated that cloud computing is an evolution in IT models, the adoption of which has far-reaching consequences. On one hand, we gain advantages such as ease and speed of deployment along with radically lower capital costs. Therefore, cloud adopters can face lower risks for new IT projects. Using a public cloud, anyone with an idea that requires IT infrastructure can act on it without actually acquiring infrastructure or hiring a staff. If you have an Internet connection, a laptop, and a credit card, you can gain access to unprecedented amounts of virtual IT infrastructure—and with a wait time that is measured in minutes rather than the weeks or months that it takes to acquire and install traditional infrastructure.

On the other hand, the downside of public cloud adoption largely has to do with the reduced flexibility inherent in public cloud services, along with concerns related to giving up physical control over information resources. And there is the *roach motel,* or lock-in, factor as well, since not all public cloud services will make it easy for a customer to move data to another provider.

Too often, traditional IT does not enjoy a synergistic relationship with other business functions. It often seems that other business departments coerce IT into bending over backward to deliver a botanical garden of unique and difficult-to-deliver or -sustain solutions. At other times, powerful IT departments push back against even reasonable business requests by either delaying or denying requests. But cloud computing is forcing change here, and the catalog of services needs to be clearly defined, as will associated SLAs. Consumers of cloud resources won't be filling out triplicate forms only to wait weeks or months for a server to be delivered. Not exactly. In the realm of private clouds, consumers of IT services will expect to get their virtual servers from a private cloud as fast as they can from a public cloud.

With these transitions and with the nature of the self-service contract for cloud services, IT will need to become a greater partner of the business overall—showing the larger organization how to get more for less. But we should also expect that the rise of cloud computing and the changes it brings will likely trend toward an overall reduction in infrastructure IT personnel. That is only natural, given the degree of automation in the way IT services are delivered with clouds.

In earlier chapters, we defined cloud computing and surveyed current cloud services and delivery models. We investigated security concerns and issues with cloud computing, and we addressed many of those by closely examining cloud security and architecture. At various points, we touched on the importance of security operations and the relationship between architecture, implementation, and ongoing security costs. This chapter is focused on the operation of a cloud from a security perspective.

The goal of operating a cloud is to deliver cloud services in an efficient, reliable, cost-effective, and secure manner. This goal can be very difficult to achieve, and it depends on many supporting activities. Architecture drives implementation and ongoing costs, including operational security costs. Efficient and secure operation is predicated on sound planning. Reactive security measures are a disruptive and costly consequence of ineffective planning. Figure 7.1 depicts this overall relationship.

Unfortunately, upfront planning and architecture are often given short shrift due to a combination of factors. One common excuse is that it is too expensive in terms of time and resources and perhaps unnecessary if you already know what you need to do. But experience generally shows that investment in

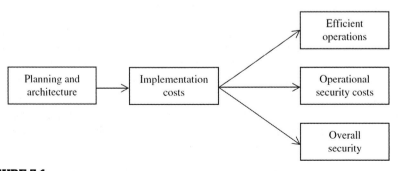

FIGURE 7.1
Overall Security and Operations Are Influenced by Many Decisions

planning and architecture can pay back savings, not only in operational costs but in protecting schedules from otherwise unanticipated issues that arise. In an imperfect world, there seem to be two choices: Spend too much time planning and delay efforts from the start, or spend insufficient time planning and experience delays or crisis later in the schedule. Rarely does a team follow a Goldilocks path.

TIP

Consider the following return-on-investment (ROI) goals for security:
- Security should reduce overall required staff time.
- Security technologies and processes should reduce overall costs.
- Security should enable functionality and enable systems management.

If we were to define some rules to support ROI for security, we might start with these:

- Security should increase revenue through increased desirability by customers.
- Security should reduce the staff time in emergency remediations.
- Security should reduce the amount of unavailable (hence unsalable) resources.
- Security should reduce the cost of indemnification (or its insurance) for breach of SLAs.
- Security should reduce the possibility of regulatory intervention, including fines and business disruption.
- Security should reduce the number and severity of public *events* that erode the customer base.

FROM ARCHITECTURE TO EFFICIENT AND SECURE OPERATIONS

Security is a key factor that is associated with all aspects of cloud operations. Long before a security engineer deactivates a former employee's various infrastructure accounts, reviews vulnerability scan results, or puzzles out which Snort events warrant concern, the efficiencies around these eventual actions are already constrained. The foundation of subsequent operational processes is cast when the architecture of the cloud is defined.

It is certainly true that a small prototype or department-level cloud can be designed and subsequently made operational with modest effort. With a small number of users and modest VM and storage resources, such a cloud will not present the efficiency demands on its operators that an enterprise-level or public cloud will. But even a prototype or department-level cloud will evidence security issues in the absence of ample planning before the cloud is made operational. These security issues can easily escalate and will demand increasing attention and resources when cloud implementations become larger.

To complicate matters, VM management alone can quickly devolve into virtual server sprawl, and valuable resources and work can become lost or destroyed as a larger cloud progresses from its initial state into an operational one whereby resource usage flexes and control is lost over virtual and even real IT assets.

Just as architecture casts the foundation for subsequent operational processes, so does the implementation and configuration of infrastructure. A cloud is a highly complex and dynamic composition that rides on various enabling technologies and components. The way these are designed, implemented, and even configured will go a long way toward enabling efficient and secure operations.

The Scope of Planning

It makes perfect sense to start the design and architecture phases of planning for a cloud by outlining the operational activities that will take place after the cloud is brought online. Planning for security operations is best done in conjunction with planning other aspects of operations. Security operations not only involve realms such as configuration management, service desk, problem management, capacity management, and service delivery, but security operations are often tightly coupled with these other aspects of operations.

The IT Infrastructure Library (ITIL[1]) is recognized for the demonstrated value it offers in terms of the detailed descriptions of the primary IT practices that an IT organization will likely face in operation. ITIL is all about capturing and organizing best practices around the full scope of IT services management, IT development, and IT operations. Hence, ITIL makes for an excellent starting point for any organization that is in the planning or early design phases of a cloud build. Of course, the focus of ITIL is on the operation and management of IT, but it has great value when we are planning and building infrastructure and defining processes that will soon form the cornerstone of daily operations.

ITIL Security Management is derived from the ISO/IEC 27002 code of practice for information security management. The goal of Security Management is to ensure appropriate information security; in other words, ensuring confidentiality, integrity, and availability of information resources. ITIL is published as a series of books, each of which covers specific practices. The overall collection is organized into eight logical sets that are grouped according to related process guidelines. In its present form, ITIL, version 2, is organized as follows:

- Service Support
- Service Delivery
- Information and Communication Technology (ICT) Infrastructure Management
- Security Management

---

[1] ITIL and IT Infrastructure Library are registered trademarks of the United Kingdom's Office of Government Commerce (OGC).

- Business Perspective
- Application Management
- Software Asset Management
- ITIL Small-Scale Implementation

Although security does have its own section, planning and architecting for security also require understanding the other areas. Going further, sound security entails mature security practices that are integrated with other practice areas. A mature and effective operations team appreciates this on a daily basis and leverages the synergies gained by cross-domain teams. In other words, when security team members contribute their expertise to multiple teams, they gain valuable understanding of activities and issues beyond security.

Physical Access, Security, and Ongoing Costs

To take operational costs to their lowest possible levels, physical access to the cloud IT infrastructure must be constrained on the basis of a documented need. Since every individual with access represents additional risk to the organization, the number of individuals who should have regular access to a datacenter should be kept low.

Unescorted access should be limited to individuals who have undergone equivalent employment screening as regular cloud staff with physical access. But even escorted access invites unnecessary risk; for example, allowing tours of visitors in close proximity to cabling, power cords, cute little buttons, and blinking lights is inviting an accidental cable loosening brush or minor outage. What is really interesting here is that when the cloud infrastructure is designed and built out for operational efficiencies, then all physical access should be fairly limited for even operational personnel—physical access simply should not be necessary on a daily basis; lights-out operations should be the goal.

Datacenters are equipped with extensive video surveillance and a foundation of environmental sensors that will detect water, smoke, humidity, and temperature. These can be further augmented with additional sensors and high-resolution cameras that can be remotely trained on critical gear to serve as a means to remotely view visual diagnostic lights or displays. Reducing the need for operations personnel to have constant physical presence will lower operations costs, high-resolution cameras are an investment that supports minimal visits to the datacenter, and the recordings from these cameras can serve as a legal record if needed. The longer the retention of video data, the better, because at least one operations team has found it necessary to review the past month of video surveillance to determine whether a backup tape was removed from an archive cage when written records were neglected by personnel.

Logical and Virtual Access

As important as physical access controls are, given that clouds are managed over the network, limiting access controls to the physical realm would be profoundly silly. No number of sophisticated multifactor physical locks or high-resolution video cameras will prevent or record operations personnel as they engage in their work managing network devices, servers, and storage devices. The use of an identity system to define and manage access by personnel to specific devices and functions is an effective way to centralize access control data. But logical controls alone are not ample to limit access to servers and other cloud infrastructure. The use of network isolation between different realms within the cloud infrastructure will go a long way toward not only limiting the reach of a hacker, but isolation will also limit the scope that authorized operations personnel have. Putting it differently: Security controls form the lowest layer of protection, and network isolation provides a second protection mechanism. These reinforce each other and provide a degree of insurance against *ham handing* configuration in either realm.

Personnel Security

Not only must physical and logical access to a cloud be limited to personnel with an operational need for access, but all such individuals must also meet personnel policies. Personnel must be screened before being granted clearance for access, access lists must be maintained in a disciplined manner, periodic reviews of continuing access needs must be made, and all operations personnel with either physical or logical access should undergo at least annual certification and refresher training. Likewise, all personnel policies and procedures should be subject to continuous evaluation, especially in terms of user access rights and privileges. When personnel leave the operations team, their access must be immediately revoked; doing that effectively entails the use of centralized identify management.

It is worthwhile adding that while personnel security is necessary it will not stop insider threats. What can be done about that? For instance, security administrators should have their work independently tested against expected outcomes. This is yet another example of the mosaic of activities that together form an ecosystem that encourages and enables security.

Training

Specific training for IT personnel is important for all staff, especially the cloud operations support personnel—which includes not only infrastructure staff but also the various administrators and staff associated with other aspects of operations. The cloud operations staff should have appropriate training to ensure that they adhere to all company policies, including security policies. With a potentially large number of virtualized servers, the potential to compromise multiple servers or inadvertently perform a denial of service is high. This will apply not just when the service is fully operational, but in the initial and ongoing buildup as well. The complexity and scope of a large cloud demand that personnel be more broadly and more deeply experienced than the typical enterprise systems administrator commonly is.

Categories of Cloud Security Staff

In general terms, the following types of security personnel are associated with the operation of a cloud:

- Physical security or datacenter facility staff
- Security analysts responsible for monitoring or associated with a physical or virtual Security Operations Center (SOC)
- Scanning or penetration-testing staff
- Security systems architects and engineers
- Chief security officer and other security management roles
- Security research analysts, security automation developers, and security content developers

TOOLS

The open-source community has embraced cloud computing in a number of ways. First, many open-source projects are hosted in various clouds. Google, Amazon, and other clouds support active development communities. Second, many open-source projects are focused on enabling cloud computing. These software development efforts include:

- *Configuration management.* These tools include Chef and Cfengine.
- *Monitoring.* Among several monitoring efforts are Zenoss, collectd, and CloudStatus.
- *Management.* This category includes OpenQRM, Bitnami, and ControlTier.
- *Cloud-enabling software.* Several efforts in this space deliver software that enables users to build, manage, and deploy cloud environments.

The cloud-enabling software area is especially active and has some very powerful tools for fielding private, public, or hybrid clouds. These tools include:

- *CloudStack* is an IaaS software platform that enables the development of private or commercial elastic cloud computing services that compete with Amazon EC2. The CloudStack platform includes a management server and hypervisor extensions to implement and manage an IaaS cloud.
- *Eucalyptus* is an open-source infrastructure to implement cloud computing on clusters and is compatible with Amazon EC2, S3, and EBS.
- *OpenNebula* is a toolkit that allows building private or public deployments and also managing the virtual infrastructure. But OpenNebula goes well beyond those use cases by supporting many different cloud models, including hybrid cloud deployment.
- *Enomaly Elastic Computing Platform* is used to design, deploy, and manage programmable virtual cloud infrastructure.
- *Ubuntu Enterprise Cloud* integrates various open-source projects (notably Eucalyptus), allowing very easy deployment of a private cloud.

From the Physical Environment to the Logical

The physical datacenter environment serves as the underlying support structure for a cloud. This is as true for a small cloud that resides in a server closet as it is for a large infrastructure cloud or for a public cloud that spans several physical datacenter locations. This physical support environment must be secure and safe if the cloud is to be reliable and secure. That alone represents a series of problems that must be addressed if power, Internet connectivity, other communications, and physical access are going to be reliable and safe.

The amount of advance planning that needs to be done for the datacenter alone is significant—in fact, it is the rare datacenter that gets all the physical components right, as evidenced by gaps that are exposed in contingency plans when things go wrong. This forms the physical security boundary, inside of which one manages the cloud enabling IT infrastructure.

Between the physical perimeter of the datacenter and this IT gear are multiple layers of physical access controls. Likewise, the typical complex computing and storage infrastructure will also evidence a number of layers of logical separation. Each of these physical and logical boundaries is an impediment to efficiency in operating the cloud, but they exist to prevent and to isolate the scope of damage that unauthorized access could otherwise lead to. These boundaries should be designed not only for protection, but also with ongoing costs in mind. Inefficiencies in design and associated operational processes will undermine the cost efficiencies of managing a highly dynamic cloud. If a cloud is going to deliver on its promises of improved efficiencies, even physical boundaries must be well designed.

Bootstrapping Secure Operations

It would be unrealistic to assume that a cloud can be operated securely without verifying the origin and security of most of the components that comprise that cloud. By example, if a piece of software to control cloud infrastructure is introduced into the infrastructure without vetting its security, we clearly risk compromising the infrastructure with malware. Since much software used today is open source, there is a real potential for installing software by downloading it directly from the Internet, without effective control over authenticity or security. That is simply not appropriate when we're building a system for production. The bottom line is that security operations depend on processes and procedures that support security—even before a cloud is placed in operation.

Efficiency and Cost

In security operations, there are several kinds of activities that consume time and yet are largely avoidable. There are other security operations activities that are not avoidable but that can be streamlined. As to the first category (time consuming and avoidable), the ability of human beings to invent unnecessary work can only explain part of the problem. Identifying, assessing, tracking, remediating, and reporting on vulnerabilities are somewhat akin to wild-fire fighting. Several strategies are possible: We can seek to reduce flammable underbrush (vulnerabilities), or we can employ fire spotters to identify an outbreak of fire. Clearly, it will be impossible to prevent all fires, but if we do not invest in some forms of prevention, we will spend more time identifying and reporting on a larger number of fires.

Every computing environment will periodically discover newly exposed vulnerabilities. Removing all vulnerabilities as they are discovered may seem appropriate, yet it is not universally possible or always reasonable. Some may be mitigated by other factors (or by compensating controls), and some are sometimes unavoidable when specific functionality is necessary. However, experience has shown that the equivalent of clearing out the underbrush in computing environments is not only possible but a best practice. What does this practice look like?

Code scanning for vulnerabilities early in the development cycle is a proven approach to reduce ongoing security costs. Likewise, developing reasonable guidelines and standards for development, for implementation, and for operations brings enduring value by preventing the accumulation of *flammable tinder* in the code base, in the infrastructure, and in operations overall. Getting back to the previous point about inventing *unnecessary work*, if we do not aggressively reduce this sort of *combustible* material in a cloud implementation, we may find that management will demand report after detailed report as to the number and kind of residual vulnerabilities and the planned schedule for remediating each of them. Isn't it wiser to avoid some problems like this to begin with?

This should be especially evident with cloud computing, where our collective desire to drive down operating costs should inculcate an aversion toward anything that leads to repeated and avoidable risk, work, and cost. It turns out that if you strive toward greater efficiency in cost, you will cast a cost-saving eye toward the cloud computing infrastructure and operations teams. And once your gaze settles on the headcount there, you should be thinking about how to not only grow your business but also to reduce your costs by making your operations more effective. Limiting ongoing costs is highly correlated with the need to avoid situations that are avoidable to begin with.

As stated, other security operations activities may not be avoidable, but many can be streamlined and made more efficient. By example, one of the periodic and necessary activities that security operations will perform is vulnerability scanning. After each scan, the results must be assessed, which involves several discrete steps, including identifying false positives. This entire process

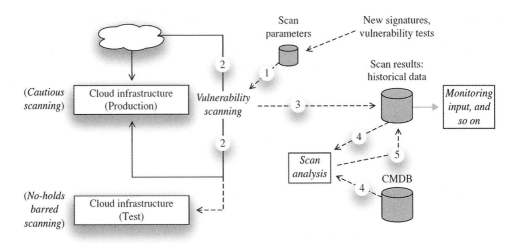

FIGURE 7.2
Managing Scan Vulnerability Data

can be managed as an unstructured series of activities, or the process can be made more mature and streamlined.

One way to do that is to generate vulnerability information in a machine-readable format or at the least in a representation that can be managed in a semiauto-mated manner. Figure 7.2 depicts such an integrated approach in managing vulnerability scan data. Note that the first step of the process is the selection of scanning parameters that are appropriate for the environment and the scan target. If the scan is to be performed against a pure test environment, the gloves can be taken off and the scanner can throw everything in its arsenal at the tar-get—since it is not a production target, destructive testing will reveal valuable information that can be applied to the analogous production environment in order to harden it and avoid a production outage. If the target has been scanned previously, it is reasonable to start with scan parameters that were pre-viously used—unless, of course, new tests are available since the last scan. As Figure 7.2 shows, the next steps are to initiate the scan and collect scan results. These results will include not only vulnerability data and associated results but also a measure of how long the scan took to run. This itself is useful informa-tion to collect over many scans as the target itself changes. The scan results are then converted or captured in a database in order to perform analysis of the current results and to assess any changes from previous results. This is relatively easy to do with a database and is otherwise too time consuming and detailed to perform effectively manually.

Once captured and analyzed, such vulnerability data is scrubbed and assessed, and it can be reported on using either canned report routines or ad hoc queries. It should be noted that the analysis that can be performed can be greatly enhanced if the database routines also have access to CMDB-managed information about the cloud infrastructure itself (as further discussed in the next section). In this manner, information associated with an IP address can be used to supply the context behind a specific alert, and an alert associated with a Web server can be categorized as a false positive, whereas the same alert associated with a directory server would be verified as critical.

SECURITY OPERATIONS ACTIVITIES

There is a direct relationship among release management, configuration management, change management, and security. However, this relationship often falls prey to sloppy procedures, a lack of formal controls, or ineffective reviews of proposed changes. CM and change control demand a degree of discipline in process that includes security involvement, not only for approvals but in planning. The earlier that security engineers are involved in planning, the less chance there is that such changes will bring unintended security risks.

Security engineers or architects can identify specific steps and procedures that can greatly improve not only security but also operational reliability. In many ways, in operations, security is a set of qualities that contribute to availability and integrity. One of the hallmarks of effective security is an economy of functionality that is best expressed by the saying *keep it simple*. Complex steps and procedures are generally not optimized, and by their nature, they present greater opportunity for error and failure. By contrast, simpler and more atomic steps can be more robust and reliable.

Server Builds

Most environments have a number of different standards for server builds. For instance, with a Microsoft Windows Server build, you may face a number of server options that start with 32 or 64 bits, and from there you may install one or more from among Internet Information Server (IIS), anonymous File Transfer Protocol (FTP) server, Microsoft Silverlight, Dynamic Host Configuration Protocol (DHCP), and Domain Name System (DNS). The options go on, and although you could have a server build with all the options installed, this does not result in a hardened build or optimum security. Having unlimited options also makes for greater operational work, so with a standard server build, you need to find a balance between flexibility and security. But this should easily be able to be kept to a small number of builds.

For a private cloud, you might want to set guidelines for the use of the environment. For instance, a set of standard operating system builds should be considered; these can be developed and tested to ensure that users can easily and quickly deploy them. These may well be a mix of Linux and Microsoft Windows servers, such as:

- Linux build: Red Hat with MySQL Server
- Linux build: Ubuntu with Apache Web Server
- Microsoft Windows Server 2003
- Microsoft Windows Server 2008

Each of these can be prebuilt and installed with the standard applications that your enterprise requires, such as antivirus, patch updates, auditing software, and so on. If you are deploying a production and development environment, these rules might be less stringent for the development environment, but any build outside the norm for your enterprise may need to be formally approved.

A brief aside about development environments: There is simply no excuse for perpetrating the disconnect between development and production environments. Cloud computing is an effective answer to this persistent problem. There is simply no reason for a development environment to be anything less than production from day one. The developers are restricted in the same ways they will be restricted in production and can manage their ways of doing things to leverage cloud advantages (such as always rolling new replacement versions of software forward and never back-patching).

Each server instance should be scaled to ensure that it falls within limits that you have set. Putting too many virtual instances on a single CPU server that all require a large CPU utilization will not yield satisfactory results. Asking the user for an indication of CPU and memory load and storage volumes anticipated without setting limits or charging is unlikely to be successful. If you offer a virtual instance on either a 32-bit platform with 2GB of memory or on a 64-bit platform with 6GB of memory, the user will likely choose the higher-performing form unless there is a cost associated. The cost needs to be sensible; otherwise, users will opt for the lower-performing instance, and this might end up causing local denial-of-service issues due to the overloaded server. The bottom line? There need to be hard restrictions on all virtual resources.

Server Updates

No matter what platform your servers run, there will be regular updates to the operating system and the applications. Operational procedures should specify how and when you perform updates on servers. Depending on the cloud architecture and the method of provisioning, you may have a lot of servers to patch. However, with a virtual environment, it makes far more sense to migrate applications from an older VM to a new updated VM. The stage is then set for proper testing of the new version before deployment, availability recovery is automatically tested, and the serious problems that regularly occur (and are always underestimated) during patching are eliminated. And it's not just the virtual environments that should be managed this way. It might take a bit longer, but automated provisioning (again, started in development) will allow the same kind of management of the base OSs and/or hypervisors.

Users and operators may well consider it easier to deploy and manage applications on an individual basis, particularly those that are known to have a defined life. At the end of life, these virtual servers can just be removed and the application terminates with no interaction with any other server. This can also make the internal cloud work in a similar manner as the external cloud by turning applications on and off as needed, which will improve the overall performance of the cloud.

As you are deploying a cloud infrastructure, the inference is that you have a relatively large number of servers to deploy. The deployment of patches will therefore require thought and discussion. The overall security of the cloud needs to be maintained, but this does not mean that each and every patch that is released has to be deployed. Taking Microsoft as an example, the company releases a set of patches on the second Tuesday of each month. These patches are rated by Microsoft as critical, important, and so on; however, the patches may be rated differently by your company due to many possible factors. Updates that are consider essential will need to be rolled out, possibly with a goal of a few days for your entire landscape of servers.

Depending on the virtualization software you are using, various automated patch management tools can be used to can enable the updating process. Using VMware (www.vmware.com), for instance, you can deploy patch management tools by VMware to manage the patching of the host and the virtual instance. If the investment you are making in the internal cloud infrastructure is for a long period of time with sufficient numbers of servers, some form of automation in the update process will likely be cost effective.

Business Continuity, Backup, and Recovery
To ensure that cloud services will be available to customers and users, we employ *business continuity*, a term that refers to a broad set of activities that are performed on an ongoing basis to maintain services and availability. Business continuity is predicated on standards, policies, guidelines, and procedures that allow for continued operation, regardless of the circumstances. Disaster recovery is a subset of business continuity and is focused on IT systems and data.

From an operational standpoint, the activities that are associated with business continuity will be woven into other operational procedures and processes, including the performance of both continual backups and data mirroring to offsite recovery systems. Creating backups should be seen as a form of ongoing insurance. Although backup data may be safely stored offsite, it may be very time consuming to reconstitute a system from such storage. What is more effective from a time-to-recover perspective is the use of multiple instances that both share the processing load but that have excess capacity to allow for any one site or instance to be taken offline, either for maintenance or when due to a service interruption. If such excess capacity is to serve as a failover capacity, the data that is associated with processing at the affected site must be continuously mirrored to such additional sites or instances.

Epic Fail

In the early 1980s, in a classified datacenter located in the Pentagon, a night-shift computer operator set about his duties of backing up a critical system. This was the day of washing machine–sized disk drives with motorcycle tire-sized removable disks. The way the backup process was designed, the system to be backed up would first be taken offline. Then a backup disk would be mounted into a second drive, and the backup program (*DSC* on the Digital Equipment PDP 11/70) was run. As DSC ran, the contents of the source disk would be copied to the target or backup disk. When the process was completed, the original source disk would be unmounted and put on a storage shelf (for backup). Then the system would be rebooted with the backup disk. The primary purpose of this system was to verify that the backup was complete and resulted in a viable copy.

Unfortunately, on one occasion the process failed, and the system could not be booted from the backup disk. Thinking that the backup had failed, the operator removed the nonbooting backup disk from the drive, replaced it with the original source disk, and attempted to boot that. This also failed. Thinking that there might be a problem with the drive itself, the operator then took the original disk and mounted it in the other drive and attempted to boot from that device. This also failed.

The operator then went to the storage shelf and retrieved the next most recent backup disk, mounted it in one of the two drives, and attempted to boot it. This also failed. The operator went back to the storage shelf and tried the same thing with the next most recent backup.

At around this point, the shift supervisor arrived and saw about 10 disks scattered on the floor. What had happened was that the original backup had failed due to a relatively rare head crash. That generation of disk drive technology was not completely sealed from dust, as are drives from the past few decades. A small hair or large piece of dust could be introduced as the disk was inserted into the drive. Since the gap between the drive heads (which float over the surface of the rapidly spinning disk) and the surface of the disk was smaller than the thickness of a human hair, a piece of hair would on occasion lead to a head crash. A head crash would physically scrape the surface of the disk platter, leaving very fine magnetic dust inside the drive.

Everything the operator did was in error. By replacing a disk that was unbootable with another one, he exposed the second disk to the same crashed heads. By switching a disk from a drive that had a crashed head to another drive, he introduced a damaged and gouged platter full of magnetic dust into the second drive, which now also became damaged. By retrieving and placing the next most recent disk and then the one older than that into the same damaged drives, the operator was methodically destroying all recent backups for the past several days.

Managing Changes in Operational Environments

A cloud provider will periodically need to revise services offerings and underlying functionality on which services are built. Before a new release can be deployed, it must be tested in as near an operational environment as possible. This can be a tall order, since an operational cloud can require many discrete components for cloud management. Such components include carrier-grade switches, routers, directory servers, security infrastructure, provisioning, and other infrastructure. All in all, the technology footprint can be extensive and expensive. A public cloud especially will not have the luxury of a prolonged outage to upgrade the infrastructure.

Several strategies can be employed in achieving a safe and predictable system upgrade. The most straightforward approach is to have completely separate development, test, staging, and operational environments. Development environments can be quite modest in terms of supporting infrastructure, but expect them to require some quality time during development—if only for brief periods—with access to larger blocks of computing and storage resources. Once a release is ready for broader testing, a dedicated testing environment will be required. Depending on the nature of the release, this testing environment may require dedicated use of some of the more expensive infrastructure—such as the ingress router or a large storage instance. However, generally the need for dedicated test environments should not entail sacrificing significant revenue-generating percentages of the infrastructure. For a private enterprise cloud, the same kinds of issues will exist, although more likely at a lower overall technology footprint.

Moving a release from testing to production will expose all manner of errors in configuration files, scripts, and procedures. Unless a release is a minor variation on a previously repeated series of enhancements, expect to run into showstoppers or debugging marathons. For this reason alone, the operations team should have at least one staging environment available where new releases and upgrades can be tested in as near to a final operational mode as possible. If the staging environment is virtually identical to the operational environment, a new release can be staged and tested with a subset of final computing and storage resources. When it is time to go live, the remainder of computing and storage can be switched over to staging in a hopefully seamless and nearly transparent manner.

But there is another set of reasons that operations really do need a staging and/ or testing environment that can be configured identically to production: security testing and scanning. Rather than performing destructive security scanning against production, it should be performed against a sandboxed staging or testing environment that, except for resources, is identical to production. The same is true for other security testing and such as may be necessary for verifying the integrity and correctness of patches and other fixes.

Release Management

Release management for a cloud is intended to ensure that proper versions of hardware and software, configuration files, licenses, and associated supporting processes are in place and correctly and reliably rolled into production. The goals of release management include effective management of all phases from planning a release to developing procedures that will be used in the rollout, along with managing customer expectations during the rollout. Figure 7.3 depicts common steps within release management and indicates the underlying need for configuration management to support a new release.

Successful release management depends on discipline in process, the use of formal procedures, and numerous checks and acceptance gateways. Figure 7.4 depicts the relationship between release management and operations, note that operational activities such as incident response and analysis can contribute to the need for changes to a cloud.

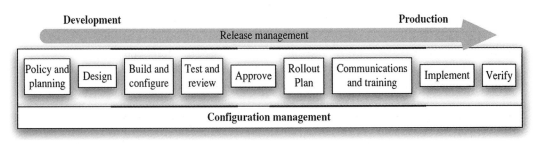

FIGURE 7.3
Typical Steps in Release Management

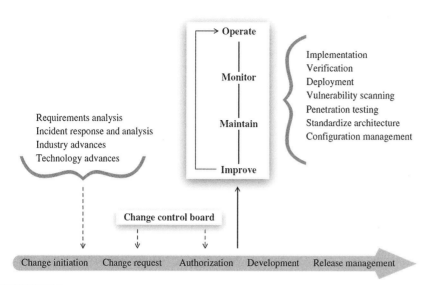

FIGURE 7.4
The Relationship Between Operations and Release Management

Releases can involve either major or minor software or hardware changes as well as emergency fixes. Emergency fixes are usually limited to addressing a small number of identified problems or security patches.

Information About the Infrastructure: Configuration Management

A complex cloud implementation will have several different categories of information about it. These will range from planning and design information to information about the configuration of the cloud to near-real-time data about the cloud. These different kinds of data will probably be found in completely separate realms and will likely have different representations.

However, because of the highly dynamic nature of a cloud and because of the greater degree of automation in IT operation, these kinds of data about a cloud should be expected to converge or at least become more accessible to management processes as cloud computing matures. Focusing on the physical infrastructure itself (the hardware that comprises computing and storage resources along with networking), one might be tempted to use a complex computer-aided design (CAD) program to represent the servers, storage, and networking—along with power cables and associated physical infrastructure. But that's just crazy—or is it? If a cloud infrastructure was designed the way complex buildings are designed with CAD systems that produce building information models, each physical element would be reflected in the model.

What would this buy you in terms of operations, and would it be worthwhile to invest in the tools and the time to develop and maintain such models? It is hard to gauge this at this point since the upfront cost of such tools is probably too high for any but very large cloud providers to be able to effectively benefit from the investment. But this notion does point in the direction of the greater control we can achieve if we have accurate and current information about the infrastructure.

Earlier, we discussed the role of a CMDB in managing knowledge about the authorized configuration of components, their attributes, and relationships. As discussed then, a CMDB offers tremendous advantages to the operation of a cloud. Not only can a CMDB be used to reflect the current state of the physical elements of a cloud, but it can enable tracking and even managing virtual cloud elements as well. The CMDB itself does not need to store information of virtual resources, but it does need to bridge knowledge and management of virtual resources to the physical and traditional CMDB realm. Doing so will enable automation in operations that encompasses the constant provisioning and deprovisioning VMs, virtualized networking, and security. To begin, the CMDB maintains contextual information about the physical infrastructure that security systems are reporting on and monitoring. Orchestration and VM management services maintain contextual information about the virtual infrastructure—what is left is to make all this information available to the security monitoring and assessment systems that are responsible for detecting and alerting security relevant situations as they unfold. Doing this will entail advances in the cloud management arena, but these advances and such integrated analysis and management capabilities will go far in further reducing ongoing operational costs, and they will bring greater security for customers. In such a view, security monitoring will itself evolve from alerting and reporting to automated security response. In a realm where attacks are automated, and at the scale of a cloud, this is necessary.

Change Management

Everything in the datacenter should be covered by a change management process, which prevents any change without correct authorization and approved. This should apply to both hardware and software to ensure that there is a smooth operation of the datacenter. A change made in one area could inadvertently affect other areas. For instance, upgrading firmware in a router may be done without realizing that some application relies on a specific firmware version. Likewise, any updates to an operating system may be required by policy but must still be put through change management, since some applications may require specific builds.

The change management process should have access to the CMDB to both verify and assess change requests and to update the CMDB after a change is completed. In this manner, changes that are made to the cloud are recorded and can be reviewed in the future for any number of reasons—including debugging.

Information Security Management

An information security management system (ISMS) is a necessity for a medium-sized to large-scale cloud. Every organization that builds a cloud of this size should have a comprehensive set of policies and procedures documents. One of the most common security certifications for a company to achieve is ISO 27002, which identifies and details the best practices for companies that are implementing and maintaining their ISMSs. Suffice it to say that the focus of this standard is the ongoing security of systems and that security in operations is a key aspect of that. ISO 27002 calls for certain activities to be in place prior to a system being operated. These activities include the following: a risk assessment, a security policy and associated standards, asset management, personnel security, and physical and environmental security. Equally important are activities that fall into operation of a cloud, such as communications and operations management, access control, incident management, and business continuity management.

Vulnerability and Penetration Testing

Penetration and vulnerability testing of cloud infrastructure should be performed on a regular basis. In many cases, operations and security personnel may not possess the specialized skills and expertise to perform these activities, in which case this may need to be outsourced to a third party. If that happens, you should ensure that the third party is professional and has demonstrable skills in this area. Although the majority of the skills and techniques used to test a cloud infrastructure are the same as testing a single application, you want to be certain that testers have a firm understanding of virtualization and cloud orchestration. Penetration testing should be aimed at the whole cloud infrastructure, not just individual servers or components. Security is only as good as the weakest link, and it is pointless if you verify the security of one server and leave others unverified. In addition, network components that enable the cloud environment need to be tested to ensure that these are securely configured. Routers and switches can have exploitable vulnerabilities, and if they are not configured correctly, they can route traffic in ways that are counter to the need for cloud security.

A penetration test and vulnerability scanning may discover a multitude of vulnerabilities, not all of which must be or can be fixed. Discovered vulnerabilities need to be graded (as simply as critical/high/medium/low). As a rule of thumb, any vulnerability that is classed as a critical or high should be remediated to ensure that the security of the entire cloud is maintained. On the other hand, low- and medium-level vulnerabilities may be accepted as reasonable risks, but this has to be determined for each cloud. Vulnerabilities that are not remediated need to have the residual risk assessed and then accepted by the business. Addressing efficiency in security operations, if you find that you have the same vulnerability across all your servers with the same build, this should be fixed in a golden image for multiple server builds.

It does need to be pointed out that many of the vulnerabilities that are discovered by scanning or penetration testing stem from poor development and coding practices. Where commercial software is the culprit, little can be done before introducing such components into an operational environment—but when the software is developed by the cloud organization itself, better coding practices can prevent the introduction of vulnerabilities into operation. This is far more cost effective than addressing poor code after it is fully developed or even in operation. Best practices here include having developers follow secure coding guidelines and security testing their code as it is developed. What can security operations do toward that goal? To begin with, operations can publish guidelines for code development and enforce acceptance tests and standards to put the responsibility for vulnerability avoidance squarely on development organizations.

WARNING

Several years ago, the author was in the middle of a customer engagement that involved developing strategies for a certain Asian government's information security modernization efforts. After several days of discussions and answering customer questions on information security topics, one of the customers asked a question that conveyed their lack of background and their naïveté. They began with: "I read on the Internet that …" The point of this is the obvious one: Don't take anything you read on the Internet (or see on TV, for that matter) as being correct or even realistic. The hype around cloud computing itself should offer ample evidence of that. Be skeptical, in a healthy, information-respecting way. Nonetheless, the Internet is especially valuable as an information resource when information is correlated and weighed in light of the source.

Security Monitoring and Response

Overall monitoring can be split into two main areas: physical and cyber. Clearly there is a security need for monitoring of a datacenter. A well-run datacenter will be fully monitored continuously and will have defined procedures in the event of an alarm. As you grow your cloud infrastructure, so too will the need for monitoring increase as well as the complexity to undertake this task. Depending on the size and location of the cloud facility, you may require extra staff and specialized equipment to be installed.

Physical monitoring will include:

- Video monitoring
- Door access
- Fire, water, and other environmental sensors
- Utility power
- Walk-through of the facility

These activities are typically the responsibility of datacenter security staff. You should have well-defined procedures in place to ensure that the logs from door access systems and video recordings are kept to meet policy requirements. These procedures should be reviewed and tested when a risk assessment is undertaken, and all the perceived physical risks should then be mitigated.

Typically, video cameras are now readily available to work across a Transmission Control Protocol/Internet Protocol (TCP/IP) network, with wireless-enabled cameras becoming more common. The way these devices are incorporated into the network is important, both from a security point of view and from the viewpoint of the network bandwidth, since video feeds are notorious for consuming large amounts of network bandwidth. If these are connected into the same network segments as data is transported over, then given a number of cameras there is a likely bandwidth contention or saturation issue. A better approach is to have a security network for all such out-of-band traffic and to prioritize traffic on that network according to site needs.

Cyber monitoring can be broken into three areas:

- Housekeeping
- Threat monitoring
- Incident response

Housekeeping

Housekeeping monitoring includes monitoring of all the servers to ensure they are up-to-date in terms of patches, antivirus updates, CPU and RAM utilization, and so on. Here again, a CMDB presents the opportunity to increase efficiencies in operation. Rather than scanning each system and identifying systems that require a patch, all version and associated information can be maintained in the CMDB itself, making for a quick search or lookup.

Periodically, it is important to verify that the CMDB accurately reflects the physical and logical environment on which it maintains information. Doing this for the entire cloud would be a daunting task, but it should be done for the components that comprise the management infrastructure. In addition, we can selectively sample and audit computing servers and VMs that are repeated hundreds or thousands of times. One way to perform a periodic audit against the logical environment is to use cataloging software. Nessus is a good example that is familiar to most security engineers. The key is to perform an authenticated scan and to collect and convert the results into a format (such as a database) that can be used to perform a comparison against the CMDB.

Threat monitoring and incident response comprise a significant security area; both aspects have to be well designed to be effective. Each is dependent on the other, and the whole process is flawed if they are not both present.

Threat Monitoring

The monitoring of the threats within your architecture will likely be a mix of manual and automated methods. At the base level, you need to collect the event and alert data from IDS/IPS sensors, antivirus logs, system logs from the various devices in your architecture, and others, as have been described in various parts of this chapter. With a medium-sized to large datacenter, the sheer amount of data would overwhelm operations personnel if they are solely using a manual method to collect and assess them. As the amount of data increases, the manual method will require a lot of extra heads, or the chance of a threat passing unnoticed will increase sharply. The bottom line is that manual methods are not in the same time domain as threats and exploits operate in, so even if they could be performed, they are simply not a reasonable approach.

Numerous automated tools can assist in this area. These tools span threat correlation engines and various security event management capabilities or systems. Chapter 6 went into detail on this topic. Basically, these tools will be able to reduce the number of false positives that appear in the raw event stream, more likely identifying more sophisticated attacks as well as alerting to any sensors that fail. The operator is thus able to concentrate on a smaller number of threats and decide whether these are real or allowed. Additionally, these tools can be tailored such that alerts are sent to the appropriate groups: virus alert to one group and failure of an IDS sensor to another group, for instance. These tools can collect data from many different sensors and then consolidate and correlate this data in one place.

The number of threat correlation engines has grown over the last few years, and there are a variety of approaches for collection, consolidation, correlation, and analysis. An assessment of these engines is outside the scope of this book; if you need one, an internal review should be held to consider your needs and compare them against the various commercial and open-source tools. The security community can also be very helpful in terms of identifying tools and relating experiences; every one of these comes with some sort of cost, and perfection has yet to be achieved.

In the past, monitoring the amount of IT that comprises a cloud would entail a dedicated network operations center (NOC) and maybe a security operations center (SOC). But today, this can largely be done virtually using secured Web-based consoles that allow a security team to operate from around the world's time zones in order to have full coverage 24/7. A NOC and SOC are still reasonable, but the scale of the infrastructure or the risk needs to justify such an investment.

Incident Response

Monitoring and detecting a potential threat is only the start. After confirming that this is a not a false positive, you need to have an incident response plan in place. This plan will have a number of different levels, depending on the severity of the incident. These will be labeled in a variety of ways—low/medium/high; major/minor; and so on—and will have an appropriate response for each.

At the lowest level, incidents can be dealt with by the operations staff as part of the day-to-day activities and will typically not need to be escalated. Obviously, these need to be tracked to ensure that there is no overall pattern and to ensure that any follow-up work (such as installing critical patches) is undertaken.

The next level of incident would be when something impacts one or a small number of servers, such as a failure of the power supply into a whole rack or network failure to one segment of your network. Although the operations staff may fix these problems, it is likely that some form of communication will need to be sent out to affected staff and tracking of the incident undertaken. Furthermore, you need to decide whether a root-cause analysis (RCA) needs to be initiated to ascertain what went wrong and whether any change to the policy and procedures, infrastructure, detection sensors, and so on needs to occur to prevent it happening in the future.

At the top level, we may encounter major incidents that affect a large percentage of the user base, or such incidents may involve a security compromise or otherwise impact our reputation. Again, planning is the key to successfully responding to such incidents. Response will often involve a broader range of people than just the operations staff and require careful and skillful management of the incident. Communications will be necessary across a range of levels, from technical to management, and will need to occur on a continuing basis.

For many incidents, it may be expedient to have a dedicated team of people who are trained to undertake incident response. This will typically be a subset of operations and management. Having a dedicated team undertake this responsibility will be especially important if the response requires that forensics be undertaken. Evidence will need to be preserved (chain of custody), and evidence can be easily destroyed or made irrelevant if the correct steps are not taken. In addition, when incidents increase from those that are easy to fix to the more complicated, you might want to have the next tier of support staff working on them to ensure they are corrected properly.

Best Practices

In the 1990s, the Information Security Forum (ISF) published the *Standard of Good Practice (SoGP)*, which identified a comprehensive set of information security best practices. This set continued to be updated until 2007 (a new version was available in late 2010). The *SoGP* was developed from comprehensive research and review of best practices around security and incident handling. The *SoGP* is often used in conjunction with other guidance or standards, such as ISO/IEC 27002 and COBIT.

In 1996, Marianne Swanson and Barbara Guttman produced the NIST Special Publication 800-14 (SP 800-14), *Generally Accepted Principles and Practices for Securing Information Technology Systems*.[1] They identified the following eight principles:

- Computer security supports the mission of the organization.
- Computer security is an integral element of sound management.
- Computer security should be cost-effective.
- Systems owners have security responsibilities outside their own organizations.
- Computer security responsibilities and accountability should be made explicit.
- Computer security requires a comprehensive and integrated approach.
- Computer security should be periodically reassessed.
- Computer security is constrained by societal factors.

These principles have enduring value and can be adapted for managing cloud security. As SP 800-14 stated: "These principles are intended to guide ... personnel when creating new systems, practices, or policies. They are not designed to produce specific answers."[2]

Resilience in Operations

Increasingly, security is difficult to define without including business continuity and governance. Where business continuity is oriented toward overcoming any substantial service interruption (and its consequences), IT governance is a form of command and control over IT. Governance aligns the business in a strategic manner to support enterprise IT evolution so that it will bring continuing and consistent business value. Governance is a process or series of actions and functions that are oriented toward delivering desired IT results.

Organizations face numerous barriers in making security into an effective enabling factor to achieve an organization's overall goals. To begin with, most systems are not really able to withstand even trivial failures without some degree of service interruption.

As stated in a report by Carnegie Mellon University (CMU):

> Supporting operational resiliency requires a core capability for managing operational risk—the risks that emanate from day-to-day operations. Operational risk management is paramount to assuring mission success. For some industries like banking and finance, it has become not only a necessary business function but a regulatory requirement. Activities like security, business continuity, and IT operations management are important because their fundamental purpose is to identify, analyze, and mitigate various types of operational risk. In turn, because they support operational risk, they also directly impact operational resiliency.[3]

One of the goals of resilience in IT is to reduce the effect of failures and disasters. Reducing the likelihood of disaster is a primary objective, but equally important is the ability to recover from disasters.

SUMMARY

Depending on how you adopt the cloud model (as a private, community, public, or hybrid resource) and depending on how you deliver cloud-based services (IaaS, PaaS, and SaaS), cloud computing brings different opportunities for change. As a new model for IT, cloud computing will be used to various advantages by competitors in the same industry, by vendors and providers of cloud services, and by consumers and subscribers.

The way an organization benefits from cloud computing will depend on how the organization assesses its present information and communications resources and how it envisions the transition to this model of computing. Already we can see this unfolding, with success being dependent on an organization's ability to grasp the opportunities and to navigate changes to existing and emerging technologies, products, and concepts—and embracing the cloud as the new model for IT.

Although private clouds can achieve immense scale and serve many internal customers, most private clouds will likely be smaller. This gives public clouds several advantages in terms of return on investment for tools and security capabilities that are inherently expensive or that require an investment in expertise to properly implement and operate.

One of the IT advantages with the cloud model is that once infrastructure is in place, most of the typical IT physical hardware and networking activities are no longer performed as a matter of course. Clearly, physical subportions of the infrastructure can be carved out—but on an ongoing basis, this is not how a cloud is cost-effectively provisioned. Cut out of the whole cloth of infrastructure, the private cloud (or clouds) and such services as SaaS, PaaS, or IaaS will be provisioned at a virtual level. From a procedural perspective, this means that the deployment and operation of a private cloud is somewhat different than normal IT operations and that you will likely need to modify existing operational procedures.

If a cloud is implemented with security along with security reinforcing operational practices and processes (from the datacenter up to expressed services), there is really no reason why cloud security can't be equal to any other implementation. In fact, as we have seen at several points in the book, due to the scale of large clouds, effective security can be far less expensive because it is spread over more tenants/users. This is due to the efficiency of scale or, to put it differently, it can be attributed to the relationship between massive scale and the lower average entry cost of better security components (from products through operational practices and monitoring).

By adopting cloud computing as a model for IT, organizations can continue to move away from more traditional device-centric perspectives toward information and services-based strategies. Clouds offer many benefits that go beyond the overall leaner IT infrastructure that they use more effectively than do other models. There are clear trade-offs that involve control over data and applications, compliance with laws and regulations, and even security. The cloud model also brings greater scalability, and by its use of *fail in place*, the cloud also brings greater reliability and redundancy. The change from a capital-heavy model of IT spending toward an operating model that is subscription-based brings new opportunities for a broader set of users and tenants to place larger bets with lower risk. Finally, the cloud model also reduces the overall energy footprint of computing, making it one of the greenest IT approaches.

The combined need for computational power, data storage, and bandwidth continues to drive demand for more highly capable systems. Data-intensive applications depend on access to increasing scales of storage. Petabyte-scale storage requirements are eclipsing terabyte-scale ones, and soon exabyte-scale storage may eclipse petabyte-scale. In addition to its other benefits, the cloud computing model makes such large-scale storage implementations more possible than is typically the case with other models.

NOTE

Some of the best Internet sources for information are sites where peers and professionals share and collaborate. Although there are many of these, there are several that stand out for cloud computing, including:

- *Google Groups.* Google, the 900-pound Internet gorilla, has provided a great and rich set of tools for collaboration among groups of individuals with common interests. The biggest issue with Google Groups is the sheer number of groups! Many of these groups have a very active membership of thought leaders in their fields.
- *LinkedIn.* This is the professional networking site with roughly 100 million professional members in over 200 countries. It is a very effective networking tool for finding and getting introduced to potential clients, service providers, and subject experts. LinkedIn groups in the areas of security and cloud computing are very active, with a broad range of ongoing discussions on numerous technical, market, and related topics. They are an excellent resource for collaboration as well as pursuing employment or filling positions in cloud computing.
- *The Cloud Security Alliance.* This organization seems to be undergoing some changes in terms of becoming a self-appointed accreditation organization.

Endnotes

1. Swanson M., Guttman B. NIST SP 800-14, "Generally Accepted Principals and Practices for Securing Information Technology Systems," National Institute of Standards and Technology, Technology Administration; 1996.
2. Ibid.
3. Caralli R., Stevens J., Wallen C., Wilson W. *Sustaining Operational Resiliency: A Process Improvement Approach to Security Management.* CMU Networked Systems Survivability Program; 2006.

Index

Note: Page numbers followed by *f* indicate figures, *b* indicate boxes and *t* indicate tables.